Contemporizing Raj Yoga

ABOUT THE BOOK

This book is meant for the 21st century practitioners of Raj Yoga. It can be used as a road map to a particular path and, the choice of a particular vehicle-method to practice with. It is the summation of their studies across four decades. The quest was to arrive at transformation of mind. It describes how consciousness → mind → brain and body are an integral whole. Even for the skeptics of esoteric practices, it provides a resolution to the dilemma as to how to integrate science and spirituality.

Well established neuroscience of molecular biology and gene expression studies in practitioners of meditation are described. The expanding exploration of the frontiers of consciousness as a quantum physical phenomenon can be glimpsed through the book.

For those with utility and bent of mind, the book is a useful handbook to find and navigate with a method that will lead to happiness. It surely will yield dividends in promotion of better health.

ABOUT THE AUTHORS

Bhaskar Vyas and Rajni Vyas are medical specialists, eminent in their own field of specialisation. They are visiting professors at the M.S. University, Department of Psychology, Baroda, Gujarat, India. They are examiners for Ph.D. at Swami Vivekanand Yoga Anu Sansthan, Bangalore Karnataka. They are convincing protagonists of mind-body continuum.

They are philosophers studying consciousness. They have studied meditation practices of Hindu and Buddhist traditions as well as teachings of J. Krishnamurty, Zen practices, Kashmir Shavism, Vajrayana and varieties of trans-cultural religious experiences. A versatile scientific training has enabled them to advanced understanding of Raj Yoga.

Being medical doctors, they are involved in the spiritual aspects of healing arts and teach these as a scientific tool in the form of hypnotherapy. And, have incorporated Raj Yoga in their clinical practices with success.

They have published over 30 + 30 papers in the National and International journals.

Their present pursuit is to integrate modern medical science with (w)holistic health.

Contemporizing RAJ YOGA

Neuroscience and Practices

Bhaskar Vyas
Rajni Vyas

CONCEPT PUBLISHING COMPANY PVT. LTD.
NEW DELHI-110059

ISBN-13: 978-93-86682-08-6 (HB)

ISBN-13: 978-93-86682-09-3 (PB)

Cover Design: **Shakti, 2017 by Rahul Gajjar**

First Published 2017

Published and Printed by

Concept Since 1974

Concept Publishing Company Pvt. Ltd.
Regd. Office:
A/15-16, Commercial Block, Mohan Garden,
New Delhi-110059 (INDIA)
T: 25351460, 25351794
Email: publishing@conceptpub.com
Website: www.conceptpub.com

Cataloging in Publication Data--Courtesy: D.K. Agencies (P) Ltd. <docinfo@dkagencies.com>

Vyas, Bhaskar, author.
Contemporizing raj yoga : neuroscience and practices / Bhaskar Vyas, Rajni Vyas.
pages cm
Includes bibliographical references and index.
ISBN 9789386682086
ISBN 9789351251903

1. Yoga, Rāja. 2. Meditation. 3. Yoga—Therapeutic use. 4. Neuropsychology. I. Vyas, Rajni, author. II. Title. III. Title: Raj yoga.

BL1238.56.R35V93 2017 DDC 181.45 23

Dedicated

To

Sri Aurobindo

Foreword

The present work 'Contemporizing Raj Yoga' –Neuroscience and Practices by Dr. Bhaskar Vyas and Dr. Rajni Vyas is a welcome publication. It is *a la novel* method for psychologists and practioners of meditation. It takes recourse to modern sciences in corroborating the ancient Indian wisdom. It aims at precise empirical certainty, intending to strike a most practical aspect in exploring oneself in realizing the perfect harmony with Nature.

The distinction of the work lies in rediscovering the hidden powers of yoga by opening up the human potential through consciousness. The yogic path is a process of evolution. It boosts the movement of nature in unfolding consciousness to a higher level. It immensely widens the human horizons from outer range of worldly levels to the inner range of the spiritual depth of man. The book is in fact a convincingly inspired work, carrying the lifelong influences of original personal experiences from *within*.

Indian thinking centred in the conviction that the authentic human life cannot be perfectly lived depending on the sole power of externalities. The life does not get its full sense until it stands *in right relation* in the higher inner spiritual being of man. The book emphasizes that all the complications of the world could not be reduced *to mere observable* apparent outer causal factors. It hints at other subtler factors within man himself for which he is normally unaware indeed! The outer skills and precisions in the studies of physical phenomena do affect their scale in the observation of inner phenomena. The fact stands that man should be aware, that he is, though small, is an integral part of the cosmic whole. The invisible accompanies the visible, even as the infinity surrounding the finite.

The reader will enjoy exploring and experiencing *the quest of RAJ YOGA* for himself. All over the world there is urgency for human unity as the only resolution in prevailing numerous conflicts. The authors have rightly hinted the need of such a synthesis of psychological ethos of both east and west in leading to such new experience and awakening of spiritual and material being possible to all.

It is difficult to describe the whole process of Raj Yoga. It has numerous variations. Raj Yoga ultimately aims at sublimation and transformation of oneself. As against this, all other forms of yoga have their own demands. The authors rightly stress this point in respect of Raj Yoga.

Nothing evolves which is not already fundamentally involved including consciousness; however veiled it may be. Meditation brings about the awakening of a new layer of awareness. It is a first sign of new awareness in man awakening to a huge 'lack' of something which neither any science nor religion nor gross hedonistic pursuits can compensate him.

It means that there are levels of consciousness beyond mind. The physical consciousness only lower levels of consciousness. There is indeed a *mind in the body* and *of the body*. Sri Aurobindo speaks of this mind as the consciousness which constitutes and operates in the formation of cells.

The present work on *Contemporizing Raj Yoga* is not aiming in reaching to the supreme heights of consciousness, but *it is in making* these highest layers of consciousness possible. The central issue is in illuminating the physical consciousness and transforming it in the light of the cosmic consciousness. That is, the sky to worldly achievement *lies precisely in the transformation* of the cells. This very transformation is the fulfillment and unfolding of yoga.

To restate, the present work is really opening up to the wider outlook to Raj-yoga. In striving to contemporize this doctrine of Raj Yoga, it gives a wider birth to various Buddhist, Jain and Tibetan yogic paths as well. This seems to be more indicating and suggesting the *universally higher locus standi* of *consciousness* than as theoretical semblance as such. The intellectual approach finds its real value ultimately only when it becomes a fact or an action and the same is rightly hinted in the book as well.

Man generally strives at many forms of disciplines either in mastering one's mind or in dominating it for a short while only. The results too are for the while and for the short duration. In the same way, each one's yogic quest too, has some unique glimpses of it. There are many vicissitudes notwithstanding; the transformation is a possibility for each one. All else do not matter more but what matters refreshingly for man is this *yogic journey as* such and sincerely following for it.

There is an address to the axiomatic question about the ultimate nature of consciousness being a quantum phenomenon. For, the *entire process of 'me'*, the subject, the object and the awareness or the observer, the observed and the observation is a complex inseparable phenomenon in the cognization of myself. The question is: Is *a virtual image* sufficient testimony to my Being? That is, my tangible form the only testimony to my Beingness? For, it is this 'I' becomes a separate entity and brings all identification as 'I' and 'not I'. This identity makes for this entire external creation into existence and observes it too at the same time. Does observation of my tangible form reduce the undifferentiated impersonal consciousness *into a locus* that I believe to be 'Me'? That is, I may therefore not necessarily be 'me' until the act of observation reduces 'I' to 'me' as restrictive kinds of conditioning, biases, complexes and limitations! That is, consciousness or self-realization may just be the 'I' discarding the images of me, going back to a fundamental state of quantum superimposition. These are quantum questions; they are answered in a flash of intuition as a non dual experience in the state of *Samadhi*.

This is how the approach with dissection from the realm of empirical inquiries remains confined to specific standpoints. That has partiality in outlook and compartmentalized in its perspective. As against this, the spiritual awakening is an unique supra rational intuition of the (w)holistic reality. The authors do point out this through Patanjali's postulates of *Ishwar Pranidhana* — a complete surrendering of the individual to the cosmic consciousness in tune with the totality of the cosmic Being in tandem with Nature. It is rather a *qualitative* inner transformation of man evolving to a higher state of his being.

In other words, the precise Indian thought in general and yogic direction in particular suggest that the 'I-consciousness' has no knowledge, it is not 'knower', barring what God designs it for his own work. This has a critical relevance in the context of the modern scientific knowledge and the lifestyle of 21st Century. This present contribution is significant in debates between matter and mind, between secularism and transcendentalism and between East and West.

Today, there is an urgent need for profound change and a deeper yearning for the spark of renewal in man all over the globe. There is suffocation with excessive materialism and alienation by robots and pervasive digital technologies. Even the east is getting uncontrolled in the same way everywhere, away from its traditional spiritual search of the centuries. Between these two extremes of materialistic skeptics and heirs of spirituality, the human life is to be fully redeemed not only from religions and philosophies, but even science and technologies. It presupposes a total and integral change of consciousness and matter and thus the *path of Raj Yoga* is a democratic spiritual leap distinct to man.

For, there has to be a change of life and existence *as a central aim of divine fulfillment.* It is not an individual achievement but a cosmic realization of the consciousness. The centralism of reasoning as of now is *veritably insufficient for human evolution.* The Raj Yoga vision is a commoners path in liberating the ego and petty compartments suffocating man. I sincerely feel that such work from eastern perspectives would rekindle a small lamp enough for the way out of prevailing darkness.

Last but not the least, it has been a privilege to write this preface. It is the sheer love and intimacy with the authors which have impelled me to humbly follow the call.

Prof. Nitin Vyas Ph.D.
Prof. & Head of Dept. of Philosophy (Retd.)
M.S. University, Vadodara, Gujarat

Previews

The book is an excellent attempt to present the ancient spiritual wisdom in a simple and contemporary way. The authors the long time practitioners themselves have given excellent practical guidance for practice of yoga and meditation...I feel a duty to recommend this book for any spiritual seeker. It is amazing as to how subtle concepts and practices have been expounded in simple way for guiding genuine seekers. The writers deserve special approbation for this.

—*Pandit Virendra Qazi*
Renowned Exponent of Kashmir School

These savants, Dr. Bhaskar & Dr. Rajni Vyas have done it once again...Deriving inspiration from there ancient Indian linkage to Patanjali, they have run parallel to swami Sivanand and swami Satyanand-medical doctors turned raj yogis in last century. This book moves a step further from enhancing creativity to alleviation and, may be, chour of certain elements.

I recommend the book to the psychologist, medical doctors for sure; it addresses the larger global audience as well.

—*Ernest L. Rossi*

During the research span extending across around 60 years. I have investigated and researched in extra sensory perception, neurophysiology & parapsychological transformation during meditation. Return back to mother India from USA, was a resurrection to me, making me realize that the answers to my quest lies in *Raj Yoga.* This domain of my research is really the magnum opus of my lifetime work.

The publication of *Contemporizing Raj Yoga* will serve to stimulate interest in scientifically studying yoga as a foundational source of a new paradigm by psychologists, and practitioners of mental disciplines. It serves the motivation and the purpose for all those who may want to study or practice. I am indeed glad to be associated with this work. I congratulate Doctors Bhaskar Vyas & Rajni Vyas for bringing out this important publication to promote yoga.

Prof. K. Ramakrishna Rao
Chancellor of GITAM University,
Ex-Chairman, Indian Council of Philosophical Research

From Esoteric Recluse from Himalayas, this treatise on *Raj Yoga* brings the Practice to the Scientific Rational, and Practice at home for every one in search of Creativity. Yoga, but has now escaped from retreats into the streets. To yoga a credible and convincing look in modern times, Drs. Bhaskar and Rajni Vyas have built linkages between the ancient yogic philosophy and practices on one hand and modern science on the other. They have touched upon several schools of yoga. The focus is on Patanjali's Raja Yoga and the practice of meditation. For scientific evidence, they have drawn primarily upon physics, neurosciences, and medicine. The book is a labour of love, and it comes through very clearly that the authors are intensely passionate about the subject.

Ramesh Bijlani
Former Professor and Head, Department of Physiology, All India Institute of Medical Sciences, New Delhi. The Chairman of Sri Aurobindo Education Society; author of *Back to Health through Yoga, Essays on Yoga*, and *A Primer on Yoga*

The book *Contemporizing Raj Yoga* is an intriguing blend of science and spirituality. The authors, Dr. V.B. Haskar Vyas a plastic surgeon and Dr. Rajni Vyas an obstetrician and gynecologist, bring to the book their detailed understanding of contemporary medicine, science, as well as indepth understanding of Indian philosophy based on the traditional yoga texts. The book includes descriptions drawn from present day neuroscience and physics to complement concepts given by the ancient sages of India. The language is clear and easy to read.

For anyone who wants to get an in-depth understanding of yoga with concepts drawn from contemporary science, *Contemporizing Raj Yoga* is a must-read.

Dr. Shirley Telles
Ph.D. (Neurophysiology), DSc (Yoga)
Director, Patanjali Research Foundation

This book contemporizing Rajyoga is amazing! I am so impressed with this distinctly different book born out of various commentaries & treatise on Patanjali yogsutra, the major text book on yoga. It is precise, concise & rather perfect; in conformity to today's world. It is completely in accordance (tune) with today's latest scientific understanding based on molecular biology, neurophysiology, neurobiology and quantum physics. Everyone will be benefitted by this book right from common people to medical fraternity to Raj yoga teachers & students. It shows ways to treat lifestyle diseases & neuropsychological disorders as well, which form majority of human ailments. In closing, this marvellous, master piece yet rather simple book is going to be a major lamp post guiding to the royal road for peace, happiness & for creative & spiritual living for one and all.

The time has come so that neurophysiology will be taught at the medical school. Practice of meditation is already being recommended as an adjunct for treatment of lifestyle diseases.

Warm Regards,

Prof. Dr. Sudhir Shah
M.D., D.M. (Neurology)
Prof. Neurology, Gujarat University, Ahmedabad

Preface

The book is a virtual transcript of the proceedings of the School of Wisdom, at the International Headquarters of Theosophical Society, Adyar, India. The first session of the School of Wisdom in November and December 2016, saw over 35 participants who came from all over the world and from different walks of life. Their motivation has inspired this book.

In 2014, the United Nations announced an international day of *Yoga* at the initiative of the Indian Prime Minister. There is a need to simplify as well as remove confusion regarding *Yoga* practices. By and large the concept of *Yoga* practice is to perform different postural *asanas*. On the other hand, the word *Yoga* means union. The union is to be established with all abounding, all pervading, ever present cosmic consciousness. Cosmic consciousness may be interpreted simply as the natural laws that govern the planet earth as well as the entire universe.

A single human being considers himself as the centre of the universe. In the pursuit of personal needs, progressing to self-preservation, an individual is likely to be subjected to stress. Stress is a generic ground for aberrant perception. This leads one to undergo different kinds of neurotic compensations. The result is dysfunction in everyday life, as well as deterioration in health.

It is but obvious that howsoever small or big a person may be, he is governed by the natural laws. Right perception results in the right action. The maintenance of normal perception, as well as smooth functioning would naturally accrue if we tune ourselves to the natural laws. *Yoga* consists of several methods whereby we unite our consciousness so as to attain a synchrony with cosmic consciousness.

Modern science has provided numerous tools to study and understand the natural laws. It has so expanded that compartmentalization is necessary. It is impossible for an individual to study all disciplines of science. When to know the natural laws in totality is impossible, a question may arise as to how does an individual cope, so as to synchronize with them. The answer is provided by classical Indian *Yoga* techniques. Apart from *Hatha Yoga*, there are other branches such as *Raj Yoga*, *Karma Yoga*, *Gyan Yoga*, and *Bhakti Yoga.* Anyone of these (with regular practice for a few minutes a day) generates synchrony with cosmic consciousness. However, we feel that *Raj Yoga* is the 'royal road' to achieve this synchrony.

The practice of *Raj Yoga* originated in India. In days gone by, aspirants were required to retreat to the Himalayas. They undertook intense penance for several years. This had to be done at the feet of a *guru* at an *ashrama*. When the *guru* was convinced about the maturity of the pupil and acquisition of definite merits, only then, say about after 12 years of penance, would he initiate the aspirant to *Raj Yoga*. After the ritualistic initiation, complete secrecy had to be maintained regarding this practice.

The 20th century saw the opening of different gates to learn *Yoga*. *Hatha Yoga* was taught across the world by celebrities like B.K.S. Iyengar. Several medical doctors turned *sannyasis* at Rishikesh and in Bihar and, imparted initiation to *Raj Yoga* with well chiseled practices. There was an advent of modern *rishis* like Sri Aurobindo, who wrote extensively and, through intense practice evolved an integration of all the branches of *Yoga* that was called Integral *Yoga*.

The scientific basis of the beneficial outcome of the practice began with Maharshi Mahesh Yogi. Being a scientist himself, he pioneered the investigation into the physiological and physical correlates of meditation. He gathered a large following worldwide. This enabled him to investigate the psychological benefits of practice of *Raj Yoga* by studying the behavioural changes. He hypothesized that meditation amounts to an altered state of consciousness (named as *Turya*—Fourth state of consciousness—described in classical Indian texts). It connects an individual to cosmic consciousness; and, Maharshi demonstrated that a large group of meditators at a single place and time can influence for betterment of humanity. This investigation continues with other scientists, some of them Nobel Laureates in Physics. Their investigations extended to the influence of mind on matter. It further progressed not only to the cohesion of functioning of both the hemispheres of the brain but, there was a second Copernican-scale revolution in emergence of a noetic psychoenergetic science. The brilliant hypotheses are in the process of verification with deductive equations. There are several well documented evidences of telepathy, clairvoyance, precognition and, a perceptible change of feelings of different vibrations at sacred places. Maybe, quantum physics has the explanations to these experiences that we may discover soon.

Molecular biology also provided scientific evidence of the beneficial effect of practice of *Raj Yoga*. The laboratories at Maharshi European Research University in Switzerland were at the forefront of this research. Candace Pert fortified the evidence with the discovery of endorphins and, further went on to discover other molecules of emotions. More than 150 information substances are now known. Emergence of bioinformatics as a new science, with the help of computation, provides voluminous information about the interconnectedness of the molecules and their variable actions. Mind intricately controls the body and, thus regular meditation can change (the molecular state dependent) memory profiles to bring about a personality change.

Scientific evidence is the currency at present. In Chapter 5 Neuroscience is discussed in as simple a manner as may be understood by a lay reader. For those who are not concerned about the scientific veracity of this ancient wisdom, may skip this chapter altogether. Even then the diction will flow smoothly.

Interest in Buddhist meditation techniques has found popularity largely because of the influence of the Dalai Lama. Herbert Benson from Harvard University travelled to Dharamshala to study the physiological changes during meditative practices and, reported his findings as the Relaxation Response. The Dalai Lama facilitated further study which enabled Richard Davidson at Wisconsin University to study the neuroscience of meditation in Buddhist monks.

This is how the doors are now wide open for the study and practice of *Raj Yoga*. Hence, strictly speaking initiation by a *guru* is not mandatory. The statement may provoke a dialectic discussion with controversy. It is to be made abundantly clear that initiation and continued guidance can make the practice of a meditator more perfect and fast rewarding. Scientific understanding can help understand and facilitate practice of *Raj Yoga*. However, peer validation, facilitation, tutoring for guidance and mentoring have, no doubt, a great importance to all students in any discipline and, so is the case with meditation. Sustained practice will realize the fruits of this rich philosophy. The last century has seen teachers like J. Krishnamurthy neither give any initiation nor did he acknowledge any *guru*. So is the case with Shri Aurobindo, Rohit Mehta and others (who emphatically denied assuming any role of a *guru* though they taught the philosophy and practice of meditation).

Some masters have made statements that meditation cannot be done; it happens. *Turya*, the Fourth state is a natural attribute of mankind. It does occur spontaneously to a select few. Most people have experienced the Fourth state for a few moments in the state of wonder, awe and any sudden appearance of luminosity either in the appearance of a charismatic personality or a panoramic aesthetic landscape. '*Aha*' experience is well documented as a sudden outburst of intuition. We suggest that meditation can be taught and *turya* can be experienced by its regular practice. Yes, one can sit down with the intention to meditate and, it happens through the steps enunciated by Patanjali. Formal ritual of initiation may have a role if the meditator believes this will enable them to better practice. This is because rituals do have a metaphoric meaning. It does tune the mind to go on to the path of meditation. If, however, there is no faith in this practice, then significance of a ritualistic initiation is practically nil.

Classical texts on *Yoga* were written in Sanskrit and other ancient languages. They are in the form of short, terse aphorisms. They were explained and expounded by scholars in the same language and the diction is full of clichés. These books are therefore, not in synchrony with present times and, are difficult to study. A departure came when Swami Vivekananda wrote pocket books on *Yoga* in English. Several philosophical works in English on *Raj Yoga* exist now. Theosophical Society published two classics: by I.K. Taimini and Rohit Mehta in 20th century. Thus, the work is voluminous.

Only originality of this work is that it is a humble aim to be comprehensive and precise introduction to *Raj Yoga*. Almost all didactic references have been omitted. However, Patanjali (the author of the *Yoga Sutra*) is primordial. The reader will find resonance with several words and phrases; and, reverberations may be felt to numerous quotable quotes. There is also some exposition to different practices of meditation such as *Vipassana* and *Vajrayana* in Buddhist meditation. Inspiration is taken from Kashmir Shaivism. Zen, from Japan, that has evolved as a novel practice, with roots in the *Raj Yoga* has also been alluded to.

During the course of study at the School of Wisdom, Mahadeva Shrinivasan expounded the horizon of quantum physics and metaphysics. The rationale was that matter equates with energy and consciousness is energy. Thus the equation can be reversible. This exposition ended with a gap in scientific evidence that still remains to equate consciousness as one of the parameters to influence matter. Kathryn Rossi presented how there can be an extension of awareness that comes through meditative practices. The enhancement of creativity and its rhythm were charted. She further explained how she combines *Hatha Yoga* with *Raj Yoga* meditation. Rupa Dave presented the work of William James. She concluded that all varieties of religious experiences have meditation as their fundamental basis. These presentations are incorporated in the text.

Tim Boyd, Chittaranjan Satapathy and Marja Artamma made this happen. Nora Simon facilitated the proceedings through out and the participants raised relevant questions. That generated insight into the needs of today. We are grateful to all of them.

We earnestly hope that the book will fulfil a need for the present times for a succinct, short and precise book that will inspire the readers to explore *Raj Yoga* meditation and facilitate their path towards an ennobling spiritual experience.

Dr. Sudhir Shah provided data about neuroimaging of brain. We wish to thank him and, take neuroscience of meditation further. Steffi Roche provided help to write and compile. Special thanks are due to Rahul Gajjar for cover page and Shivani Vakodikar for illustrations. We wish their *Tapa further* fructifies for them to be a *Raj Yogi*.

21st June, 2017,
3rd International Yoga Day

Bhaskar Vyas
Rajni Vyas

Contents

Contents

Chapter 1

Development of Personality and Social Coherence

We begin by paying homage to *Rishi* Patanjali. Patanjali is antiquated to 2500 B.C. His exposition of *Raj Yoga* is in eight steps. It is classical. The original text is in four chapters with 196 euphuisms. The eight steps are:

1. Social and cultural norms in a civilized society.
2. Personal norms that should become standard rules for character and personality.
3. The postures for meditation.
4. Breathing practices.
5. Disconnecting from sensual impulses from all—Six senses.
6. Focalization on a sound; *mantra* and/or a visualization that is portent with symbolic meaning.
7. Beginning of the experience of an immersion of one's self into the focalized *mantra*, or visualized symbol; dissolution of the separateness of the meditator, and the object meditated upon into a singularity.
8. There is Void (*sunyata*), devoid of duality. That is *Kaivalya*. That Alone is.

The steps narrated this way are in a format sequence but need not be followed seriatim. The steps will be explained to suit the sensibilities of modern times, so as to come to a better understanding. Moreover, this is a (w)holistic study of meditation practiced in diverse forms. Therefore, the text is synchronous with Patanjali's text. Moreover, we discuss various dimensions of *Raj Yoga* that emerged and are still unfolding, including Buddhist meditation and hypnotherapy (!).

MOTIVATION TO MEDITATE

At the onset we need to understand the need for *Raj Yoga* meditation.

Every human being has needs and wants. These are desires and aspirations. They revolve around satisfaction of personal needs that occur from basic shelter and hunger to sexual satisfaction, accumulation of wealth, acquisitions and attainments that progress to acceleration of merits and fame. Every person wants to be happy and, in addition there is an instinctual need to be distinguished. In addition, there is an aspiration to evolve to a higher state of being. In order to fulfil this particular subtle need there are well charted paths that we call religions. The masses consider religion as a word by a personified god or his messenger or a prophet. When the belief in the god is denied, a word spoken from the sky is substituted. With this belief that has been propagated for centuries, a particular region of the brain has evolved that regulates religiosity. All religions are pathways to sublimity; when practiced with humility. When followed with dogmatic emphasis that there is only one path and, no other religion can correspond, it has created conflicts in the world. However, a truly religious person following the dictates of his own belief can live a life of equanimity and peaceful happiness.

The social structure since time immemorial has revolved around competition and collaboration. Towards the fulfilment of goals, who should get what, how much in what particular way at what particular location and time and how, are the questions that political *pandits* keep on discussing. Marxists, Capitalists and political philosophers have created a cold war for decades. One or other kind of strife towards the exclusive gain towards a group or country continues.

PERSONAL STRESS

What is thus evident on a large scale of human endeavour is experienced by most people in personal life. Competition is experienced as a challenge in most of the spheres of the activity. Out of this stressful situation, a reflection both on body and mind is created. It is a continuous self-propagating effort at self-preservation where the end result is either fight or flight. This is well defined as stress response and, has been studied in depth at psychological and molecular levels.

The stress situation causes clouding of the perception. Right action and behaviour that is conducive to happiness comes through the right perception. In a stressful state, the perception is vitiated through irrational and extraneous considerations in favour of self. The actual situation is coloured by the neurotic projections of the mind, which wants to derive the compensation for it. This may denigrate the reality to the extent of a total denial of actual. A situation arises where the person is in constant strife to balance between the personal self-preservative instinctual needs and constraints imposed upon by the normative standards laid down by the society.

The dialectic discussions, divisive compartmentalization and dissections are the logical processes through which the mind drives to define the alternatives. Critical thinking may lead to correct choices, yet; even highly logical processing by intellectualization is not necessarily conducive to the expected harmony. Though brain processes logical thinking in mathematical, algorithmic processes, even with iteration, it has the tendency to make certain choices and omit facts in human situations and relationships. This may lead to a chaotic condition of mind. The well-defined concepts may get blurred and a wrong judgement may lead to a personal disaster.

DOMAIN OF SPIRITUALITY

In contrast to logical functioning by the left half of the brain, the right half functions in a different mode. Instead of linear algorithmic sequential processing, it takes a composite spatial (w)holistic situation into account. Right brain provides answers through an intuitive process and avoids arguments. It is the domain of spirituality. The present day civilization is pushing through the achievements through the dominant activity of the

Table 1.1: Characteristic of Left and Right Brain Activity

Left Hemisphere	*Right Hemisphere*
Speech/Verbal	Spatial/Musical
Logical/Mathematical	Holistic
Liner, detailed	Artistic, Symbolic
Sequential	Simultaneous
Controlled	Emotional
Intellectual	Intuitive, creative
Dominant	Quiet
Worldly	Spiritual
Active	Receptive
Analytic	Synthetic, gestalt oriented
Reading/Writing/Naming	Facial recognition
Sequential ordering	Simultaneous
Perception of facts	Comprehension
Significant order	Perception of abstract
	Pattern
Complex motor sequences	Recognition of complex figures

left brain. For a mature functioning of the intellect, a collateral functioning of both the hemispheres of the brain is required.

The personality develops through the fulfilment of hierarchical needs such as food, protection for the future, affectionate relationships and love. Most people then strive for esteem. The ladder is built in a milieu of uncertainty and conflict. The motivation should be oriented, as to be what the person is actually made to be, rather than a continuous effort at becoming what may be an elusive or a delusive ideal set by the environment. The proper choice made in such a state, will lead to peace and happiness. Meditation practiced by any method, provides a comprehensive technique of resolving chaos developed in the mind through such conflicts. Meditative way is the royal road.

MEDITATION: ROYAL ROAD

Purification of Mind

The meditator has to prepare by observing a certain norm for formatting his character and refining the personality. Not only a physical cleanliness is elementary; one must constantly endeavour to purify the mind. Mind is a mirror that constantly gathers dust. It needs to be cleaned so that its reflection is not jarred. This may be done with a prayer of choice or a prayer combined with a ritual. Classical Hindu rituals are further standardized at the Theosophical Society as *Bharat Samaj Pooja*. There is systemic step by step purification of the mind with its several components. Indian philosophy has an expanded version of mind that radically differs from the Western. It includes the personality. In this preparatory stage, there may be a spontaneous transition to focalization. During the process one may visualize a temple being built that spontaneously merges with the meditator at the end of the ritual. The steps need to be followed as a way of life thorough out.

***Satiety* (Santosh)**

The suffering is real. The cause of suffering needs to be identified. It can be easy when it is obvious or, one has to delve deep in the unconscious mind to identify so as to remove it. One of the commonest ways that suffering is inflicted is uninhibited ambition. When a bird aspires to be a flower or when a moth toils to become a star, it will simply burn out itself. Mother earth has enough for everybody's need but greed cannot be satiated even by the bountiful bestowment. Common causes of stress are extended hours of hard and not enjoyable work with a view to acquire more and more possessions. Most disputes and conflicts arise around wealth. Social fabric is woven around trade and commerce; that shall go on in any society. When the greed creeps in, dishonesty is likely. In the pursuit of more acquisitions—and here even unbridled acquisition of merits and excellence may also be included—time contracts and happiness is compromised.

The resolution is simple. The key is in finding satisfaction with what we have and what is gained, as of today. What is left undone as of now, there will always be a tomorrow to do it. And the argument is extended that if not in this life time; there will be a next birth. And, if there is no re-birth, how does it matter that something was left unfinished?

It is said that ambition generates growth and prosperity; this is indeed true within a judicious living. One should save for a rainy day and a brilliant person should pursue excellence, but this should be done with a pause. Even in the neuronal transmission at synapses in brain and other parts of nervous system, there is a minimal time gap—pause—while the information is relayed. In the creative process, a pause provides the time for processing the data. Thus being satisfied in the present moment creates a mental state of joy and enjoyment at work; thus eliminating anxiety and worry. Look at the child suckling the milk at the breast of the mother: hunger once satisfied, it gives of the nipple and falls to sleep!

Sustained Effort (Tapa)

For a person in 21st century, with motivation to be a better human being through meditation, it is not necessary to go to forest or to mountains, and to make intensive efforts for years by standing on a single leg. Aspirations are deep rooted in the built up of personality. In contrast to ever jumping ambitions, aspiration may be embedded into the genes: so that there is a subtle ticking of the process akin to metamorphosis without constant strife. The growth is then a process as it happens in morphogenetic fields and, takes place, without the strife of achievement of milestones within a time frame.

Intense effort is not just one time performance. Most difficulties in life situation arise out of faulty understanding of inter-personal relationships. Either one has acted with an incorrect response to misleading information or, has failed to exercise lack of control to others misbehaviour. One has to perform introspection and identify ones own weaknesses. Only then one can respond with discretion to the threats from outside. Discernment is a must so as to, not to fight; not to flee but just flow in response to stress. And yet, to strive, to struggle; not to find and even then, not to yield; Romain Roland said poetically so across the continents, from France.. This is *Tapa.*

Man lives in a society. It is impossible to have control over the actions of the people in the surrounding. Therefore, to live peacefully, a simple way is to have control over one's own self and, act accordingly. Self control is exercised by sustenance and preservation of vigour and physical strength, parsimony of speech and, control of mind from wavering and wandering; this is *tapa:* it is said so in *Bhagvad Gita.*

This effort is a life long pursuit till it becomes natural.

Self-Study (*Swadhyaya*)

Thus a steady routine of constant review and revision is a necessity for balanced life style. Critical assessment of the environment and learning would show a need for further refinement. Meditation learnt in whatever way, even may be with an initiation by a guru can just be a conditioned process. The expansion of consciousness in the meditative process is unlimited. It is further enriched with refinements learned by continuous study. There is no end goal in the process and a continuous steady progression without the set milestones occurs as *happenings*. The help can further be extended with right choice of friends. There may be a deliberation through dialectics or simply extending of notes within a harmonious group. Synchrony is a must.

Graceful Acceptance (Ishwar pranidhana)

Such an endeavour is a joyful effort. The accomplishment results in a pleasant personality that toils without creating stress. Aspiration for excellence has to be combined with intense effort. It requires an unwavering mind and a determination to persist. Then, work becomes worship.

However, for an overall development, equanimity is necessary so as to accept mistakes and failures. A positive mindset is cultivated and intense effort has to be applied joyfully. The methods and strategies have to be carefully worked out and the perception cleared of neurotic defenses. Even then, for reasons that may or may not be understood, there can be a failure. It is beyond human capacity, to be in total control of all that happens. Non-accomplishment of a goal within a particular time frame must be evaluated differently. There could be a revised effort at a different time frame with peaceful acceptance. There is no need to cry over spilt milk. A graceful acceptance of the fact will save the energy to pave the way differently. The results of a particular effort are determined by who is doing it, what is being done, the time and the situation where it is done. The motivation as to why it is done, also affects the end result. However, even after a careful application that should ensure a well predicted result, there may be a failure. This should be gracefully accepted without any remorseful punishment inflicted on the self; Let thy will be done!

A spiritual life style is bereft of strife. But life is a movement: any movement will involve some friction. Cultivation of certain positive attitudes to the thought processes generates an approach to spirituality. Attitudes lead to behaviour; and, behaviour reflects how and what does a person think. In addition to what is said before, Patanjali emphasizes four qualities that encompass cognitive process—psychodynamics, and behaviour simultaneously. Finally, these qualities shape the personality. We shall examine them now.

Attitude of Friendship (Maitri)

While it is true that a human being is the product of a particular genetic makeup, it is wrong to believe that the character cannot be cultivated. There is constant up and down regulation of genes. Sensibilities can always be refined and further excellence can always be achieved. Rather than perceiving the environment as a hostile force, it is useful to see it as a contributory factor for personal growth. An attitude of friendship with everybody around must be cultivated. Enmity arises out of conflicting interests. There is no fundamental enmity—it is only a conflict of interest—and such notions should be wiped out by understanding the motives of others. To understand others and thereby, forgiving all, is altruistically true.

It is especially difficult to practice forgiveness when a grievous hurt is inflicted by someone. Similarly, it can be arduous not to be able to forgive even a small mistake by oneself; requiring a careful endeavour to ignore and not ruminate over the deficiency of others as well as oneself. No human being is perfect. Reacting to others creates hatred, jealousy, enmity and such negative feelings. Reacting to one's own mistakes will produce autoimmune diseases.

It is not possible for most and, difficult even for the erudite to psychoanalyze the motives of crooks, manipulators and villains. It is naive to deny their existence. When a spiritually oriented person relates socially in the spirit of friendliness, he is perceptive of corruption. In such a situation, the solution is simple. Missionary zeal to reform the evil should be restrained. Everyone is entitled to free will; a wise is choice to disengage, or what action to follow comes out intuitively through meditation. Meditation will wipe away confusion and despair and generate spiritual qualities.

Compassion (Karuna)

A spiritual person is full of kindness and compassion for everyone around. He is aware that suffering does exist and tends to offer unconditioned help to those who are deluded in their perception or distracted towards false aims; and, also for those who are suffering because of a disorder. Such an outlook produces a sense of belongingness and is conducive to harmony.

The harmonious relationship is further facilitated by the development of an attitude of appreciating the merits and virtues of others. As nobody is perfect, in the same way, most individuals have some merit of whatever kind. Recognition and acknowledgement of a particular merit makes the individual happy. Thus there is a cyclic relationship between the cultivation of faculties for friendliness, in ignoring the faults of others or pardoning their mistakes, with a kind compassionate attitude so that the virtue in others is brought to the surface. Cultivation of such a mentality gives an individual a charming personality that relates with compassionate kindness and charity to all.

Appreciation of Virtue (Mudita)

Every human being is endowed with certain merits regardless of education, status and position. The focus is to connect to those qualities and, appreciate the individuality rather than valuation as a tradable commodity. Appreciation of positive sensibilities of a person brings about a sense of being wanted and bonding develops. This will be fundamental to a lasting friendship devoid of competition. Even when no interconnectedness is involved, a benign "live and let live" environment prevails socially.

Disengagement (Upeksha)

On the other hand, no individual is perfect. Frailty is also a basic attribute of humanity. To err is human. It is hard to spot a person who has not made any mistake. People make unintentional blunders; that may be just accidents. A persistent lack of etiquette, misdemeanour or uncouthness may be culturally conditioned. Arguing, making issues and taking a stand on small matters, howsoever right, may just end up in being frivolous. To gloss over such situations and move over to productive work prevents wastage. A person with large understanding and in depth wisdom understands the limitations of persons with lesser abilities and limited faculties. Faults may be passed over in a spirit of friendship and, ignored.

Or some one may be just mean; to disengage with the mean-minded and manipulative people is wisdom. Freedom is most valued quality of civilized society; choice of disengagement is available to all. With malice to none, but choice of freedom to disengage with energy draining people and processes, sparing of energy for creativity will thus ensue.

COHERENCE WITH SOCIETAL NORMS

We have observed the importance of cultivating certain personal values. We now move over to the observance of norms that are imperative for the smooth functioning of an individual within the society.

Truthfulness (Satya)

Truthfulness seems to be elementary; it is even more fundamental for frictionless function. The relationships rest on mutual trust. While there cannot be an obsession about truth in trivial matters, say telling the exact time to the dot, almost all social transactions rest on promises. Vows have to be kept. Relationships get frayed due to manipulations to twist language and twist intentionality. Meanings of words are meant as per the meaningful promises and they should be fulfiled as per the meaning, which was meant to be conveyed by the parties concerned.

Ethics are for ever; ethos of a social structure keeps on evolving with times. Truth can only be One; and, quest for Absolute truth, that is eminent, changeless and everlasting is a on a pathless land. Meditation unveils the chart of route and location for landing.

Non-Violence (Ahimsa)

Avoidance of physical violence is a well-established norm in all civilized societies. An aspirant may enlarge upon the meaning of non-violence so as to be as gentle and forbearing in everyday life. While speaking, even harsh words and emphatic, forceful denials should be avoided. Parsimony in speech can drive the point and, saves time. This will be conducive to smooth relationships and ease of transactions.

Non-Stealing (Asteya)

Stealing is a crime; however, there is widespread stealing in covert forms in the society. What is not ones own and, belongs to someone else, howsoever small or big, has to be returned. What is not earned with right means is a theft from society. This can cause even social upheavals at a great personal cost. An attitude of contentment is an effective tool against temptation to stealing.

Non-Accumulation (Aparigraha)

Accumulation is a dominant trait in the affluent society. We tend to not give away unnecessary possessions and, caring for the accumulated possessions is burdensome. It may be asked, how about the habit of savings for the householder. Saving is a necessary habit for every family. A certain savings is necessary to carry out future responsibilities. This should be done in a spirit of trusteeship and, is a virtue that is deeply rooted in human psyche. A careful exercise in holding the wealth in trusteeship for betterment for the social needs, justifies the capitalistic ideology. Its culmination into philanthropy is a just compensation.

Restraint from Excessive Pleasure (Brahmacharya)

Celibacy is wrongly interpreted as avoidance of sex. Sexuality is a basic human instinct. Sublimation of sex drive is possible for a few selectively ordained to be special; for most householders, it makes for a family and, ensures a future generation. Restraint is necessary in all walks of life and, restraint is not to be forcefully enforced. When there is a graceful acceptance of one's portion, out of natural circumstances and the enjoyment is limited to that only; the pleasure seeking comes to a halt with joy and delight pervades all activities. While enjoyment refreshes, its excess causes stress. All stressful situations blur the perception and cause a burn out of bodily systems.

TEN COMMANDMENTS

We have named ten pillars for character building that almost corresponds to Ten Commandments in Bible. They are so acclaimed in numerous, various religious texts as primary requirements for pilgrimage on the meditative way. That leads towards the achievement of realization that there is no difference between Cosmic Consciousness and consciousness of the individual's meditative self.

Those who may have had an opportunity to sit at the feet of a master are indeed fortunate. However, this way of life may be imbibed through self study by reflection and reasoning as well. Cultivation of qualities of discriminative wisdom, leads to a state of desirelessness, so that, to be devoid of the desire of being desirelessness is also abandoned. The study generates a ground of performance of every choir of life with compassionate kindness comparable to love for all; not only people, living beings, including plants and trees but, also environment.

It may be argued that these are well-established virtues for normative functioning of the society. The societies have observed them since time immemorial and, all the ten pillars for development of a spiritual personality and sustenance of societal structures are elementary. It is to be emphasized, that by strict compliance to them, not only in personal life, but across the globe, great social and political upheavals could have been avoided.

MAHATMA GANDHI: A SINGULARITY

We take just one example in Mahatma Gandhi. Mahatma did not formally do any meditative practice; may be he meditated on the spinning wheel. Only by a masterful observation of the ten principles, he came to develop a charismatic personality that brought a silent revolution amongst the masses, not only across

India but, also across the globe. Most of his important decisions were inspired by intuitive insights. He said, "My life is my message": that translates that *Karma Yoga*, also generates intuitive insights when the work is done with full compliance of Ten Commandments of Patanjali.

THE DALAI LAMA: A SINGULARITY IN REVERSE

Alternately, the Dalai Lama is a living testimony to what meditation may do to the personality in shaping. He was separated from parents at a tender age, to be housed in Potala Palace, had to face and flee from Chinese, even after being enshrined as a Sovereign to live as a refugee in India, being accommodated and admonished by Pandit Nehru. He went on to be a Nobel Laureate for Peace and, has been welcomed. Now, he has emerged as one of the most respected personage of our times, conducting *Kalachakra* initiation for hundreds of thousands who flock to him from across the globe. Evolution of such nobility is not a mere accident; it has bearing in the history. Around sixth century A.D., a Buddhist monk named Paramsambhava crossed over the Himalaya to Tibet. As a part of Buddhist religion, he carried *Vajrayana* meditation with him. This is rooted fundamentally in meditative practices from India. The Dalai Lama mastered *Vajrayana* practices at young age, and still is advancing by practice and teaching spirants to *Kalachakra* initiation.

ENDS AND MEANS

Some find it difficult to meditate as they do not experience trance. For them even practice of the elementary virtues as discussed, may suffice to carry on a smooth and purposeful functioning. The debate about deployment of dubious means towards "noble ends" is indeed futile: right means are the right ends. The first step is the last step. With constant endeavour to be self-righteous, people may develop the faculty for intuitive insight as well.

It will then augur well for journey on the spiritual path.

Chapter 2

Mind and its Manipulations

Meditation is a state of freedom of 360 degrees; there is no need to be structured by any format. Whatever construct is given here is for narration. There can be choice to begin from any step.

Meditation is a spiritual experience that comes about through a paradigm shift in consciousness. An attitude of faith in natural laws, and, trusting the wisdom of the sages needs to be compounded with energetic drive. It is brought about through an intensity of pursuit. However, a clear and succinct memory constituted with intelligent processing of the meditative experience needs to be practiced.

Meditation brings about an altogether different approach in daily pursuits. To begin with the practice, one may face obstacles. The distractions could be a casual approach or doubt in the practice itself. Mediation is a pathless land though several charts abound. It is without material gains and, there is no goal scoring. When certain desired goals are put as a benchmark, their non-attainment would waiver the practitioner to put off the practice. This can be obviated with persistence. For a beginner to cultivate a one pointed attention may be difficult. It is useful to recall the memory of even a few moments of intense happiness and pure joy experienced during the altered state of consciousness. This will motivate one for regular practice. Gradually, steadiness of the mind will accrue with refinement of aesthetic experiences. The tranquillity, the calmness and clarity in perception will further motivate the practice.

However, we should initially understand the structure of mind.

STRUCTURE OF MIND

While one is constantly minding the mind, we wonder, what the mind is. Mind has no matter. It is a product of brain functions. It is to be understood (w)holistically that environment, brain, endocrine glands, autonomic nervous system and the cells all over the body, with their 150 + cytokine secretions create a state dependent memory profile—a panorama. That is on constant record for all the time as various layers of memory. That is mind: the psych, its functioning is psychodynamics.

Mind is frequently confused with consciousness; and several hypothetical-philosophical structural models are postulated. *Rishis* and *pandits* coin new words for describing different mind states. Sri Aurobindo used the word Overmind that corresponds to Fourth State—*turya*. He postulated yet another higher state, calling it Supermind. That equates with Cosmic Consciousness, permeating the entire universe.

It is useful to work with academically well defined definitions of mind in the initial stages. There are three layers of the mind: conscious mind, sub-conscious mind and unconscious mind. Usually, we think with conscious mind. Sub-conscious mind recalls a few of the facts with some effort. But mind is like an iceberg; 90 per cent or more of it is submerged. This is unconscious mind and, usually it cannot be recalled to awareness. It is deeply submerged with a psychodynamic process—repression. It is generally not available to memory and yet it exists. During the process of meditation the lid to the unconscious mind is opened. This should happen gradually.

The unconscious mind is the drive behind most behaviour patterns of the individual. When the contents of the unconscious mind are laid open the steam of repression is let out. Unravelling the unconscious mind may allow the repressed memories of traumatic events to surface. This may be truly disturbing. It would be advisable at such a point to seek guidance as to how to proceed further. A tranquil observation of the contents, in a state of equanimity produces insight as how to get rid of neurotic compensations that one may have resorted to cope with the stress. It should be emphasized that psychiatric diseases like obsessive compulsive disorder; schizophrenia etc. also have their causation deeply rooted in unconscious mind. Meditation should be avoided by them. But for the rest, meditation is a panacea. Yet it will need the generation of in depth insight to get rid of a traumatic childhood experience. The victims of purposeless desires for unnecessary wealth and fame will immediately gain insight.

PSYCHODYNAMICS OF DEFENSES OF EGO

Ego is a psychological entity that equates with our notion of our self. For most of the time, the mind functions in the service of the self. For the mind, "me is that what I call myself". The ego constantly strives to balance between the irrational demands of id, over the restrictive demanding commands, to confirm to the social norms, by superego. This puts the personality of an individual into a delicate balance that can be tipped off by challenges to the self-interest and self-preservation. Stress is thus widely prevalent in the present social and civilization structures across the individuals at various stages of life.

VITIATED PERCEPTION; PSYCHOANALYTIC PERSPECTIVE

Stress situation bring about various kinds of neurotic modification in the perception of a situation. Neurotic defenses serve as means to view the situation, in favour of oneself. Ego tends to be narcissistic in an unfavourable situation. It projects and uses projection so as to blame an unreal situation, even one's own impulses; to the environment or the people other than oneself. This may progress further to an altogether denial of an existing situation. Thus a person may have normal vision but would refuse to acknowledge what is seen, there might be a loss of hearing with normal ears. This is a hysterical behaviour.

One may grossly redefine the perception of external reality to suit the inner needs, so that reality is totally distorted. Distortion may grossly reshape the external reality, to fulfil personal needs of superiority over others and, that may extend to megalomania. Such a person constantly battles with others, so that his politics are primarily aimed at self-serving and pocketing the largest possible portion for himself.

Such faulty perceptions lead to manipulations. These may involve acting out and behaving in a dramatic fashion. Such theatrical behaviour would extend to blocking out the affect and even rational critical thinking. Failure to achieve the selfish goals through such manipulative behaviour may lead to hypochondriasis which is a prelude to a real physical illness.

A perpetual neurotic endeavour leads to further distortions of perception. One may get unnaturally attached to the objects and subjects of affection around, so as to introject them as a part of one's personality. When this is insufficient to sustain the stress, ego uses displacement by purposefully shifting from one object to another. These actions relieves stress, by putting it on hold for a while that may lead one to an altogether different direction in life. Thus, shifting the activity of interest may resolve in solving a conflict: however, there is displacement of goals.

A constant struggle to cope with stressors may bring about a drastic modification in personality of the person. Avoiding emotional distress may lead one to dissociate so as to be dysfunctional. This may be compensated by intellectualization. Rational analysis and critical inputs from peers and mentors with sophisticated intellectualization may restore rationalization. Thus immature neurotic behaviour, through a process of logical sequences can be corrected and, restore the personality.

Everyone wants to be in full control of oneself and the surroundings. Highly stressful situations may jerk entire personality of an individual. One can understand or made to look at situations in this manner; one may lose a book and could replace it; by spending some money: one may miss a bus and would have to wait for the next; spending a few minutes: trains when missed will make you want to rush or run for it which is dangerous; however, within a while or a bit longer, another one will take you to your destination. Highly emotional situations like a loss in love or huge losses in finances and prestige cannot be remedied by such kind of mere counseling. A legend or a fallacy may be constructed in the defense of oneself so that analogies, similes and metaphors are employed by the individual to cope with the stress. However, this may lead to isolation of the individual from friends and the society. This leads to a reactive tendency which may cause an abreaction. A sudden awakening to the correct perception of reality through some abreaction may occur, but only for a short time. This would not eliminate the tendency, but may bring about repression into depths of unconscious mind that may keep on reverberating from time to time.

An ascetic tendency is not unusual in Indian culture; even altruism abounds as a way of life. However, even in any culture or society that derives its drive primary from ego satisfaction, there would certainly be people who have imbibed such noble qualities after some frustrating experiences. Absurd it may sound, but some of such instances may also be in service of survival of ego!

However, a person who has made meditation a part of his daily life, is unlikely to go through such stages. He/she will not need an intervention or counseling. Yet, a word of caution is needed. Even a slight opening in the window of the unconscious mind will bring out several bizarre ideas. If any of this idea dominates the mind, meditation will not progress; even psychological derangement may happen.

There is no certainty as to when and how does consciousness arise in a fertilized embryo; but there is evidence to suggest that within a few weeks, the foetus develops brain and, the brain starts developing a mind of its own. Foetus derives sensorial inputs from the surrounding and labels it with basic instinctual interpretations. Phobias and fears, anguish and anxiety, faith and angels may have their deep roots in the psyche of foetus. This gives some idea as to how difficult it may be to wipe the mirror of mind clean.

We have thus observed, as to how a mind would normally function and its various dysfunctional tendencies. Classical Indian concepts are much more elaborate. We shall discuss them appropriately in chapter 7 while studying the progression of meditative process.

With a view to progress with a single pointedness to meditation, one has to develop a faculty to be not be distracted by the disturbances. Proceeding to the meditative stage in a step wise manner is conducive to a calm, cool, composed manner. When the experience of Fourth State occurs, it will be gentle and generate a state of well-being and happiness. Let us now further examine the process. For a smooth progress we shall understand a bit about consciousness.

Chapter 3

Meditative State Transformation through Trance

Having understood what is mind and how it manipulates perception, we need to further understand consciousness. Mind operates usually in the ordinary awake state. It surfaces during dreams in the form of metaphors. And, as we have seen, unconscious mind is a demiurgic dynamic force that motivates most actions. Meditation ultimately progresses to a state of choiceless awareness; past memories and future projections cease to be. Ultimately, it quiets the mind to the extent that it may even vanish. Yet, consciousness, of a transformed kind persists; so obviously mind and consciousness should be understood as different.

TRANSFORMATION THROUGH TRANCE

Mind is full of thoughts as we have understood. Meditation brings about a total cessation of all thought processes. Entire ideation ceases. It is comparable to zero state of computation in a computer; there is no activity and, yet the basic programmes are subtly active. Consciousness persists; but the entire mind with its corruptions is erased. It is a new mind; a clean mirror. Some philosophers poetically call it a mutation of mind.

This occurs through a transformation through the trance in Fourth State. A transformation has occurred: that itself is a new creation. And, creativity flourishes with regular practice of meditation. Therefore, let us understand about various states of consciousness.

COSMIC INTELLIGENCE

We may have hardly thought as to how consciousness arises, how does it transform and how, and where does it vanish at death. At some stage of biological evolution living organisms came into existence and, the matter came to manifest consciousness. Then it must be intrinsically contained within matter. If the implicate order of the matter is to incorporate consciousness, one has only to find the tools by which implicate, encoded order becomes explicit and unfolded into consciousness. The logic is simple. Yet, consciousness is still a mystery. It cannot just manifest as self emergent quality of matter. Instead, Classical Indian tradition postulates that consciousness—cosmic intelligence came first. Philosophers of science also believe that at Big Bang, the first happening was a beginning of cosmic intelligence: subsequently that formatted the matter in the universe.

Expressing itself in the form of self-conscious, personal existence, the consciousness in man is in constant interplay with the phenomenal world. Awareness may be of ones surroundings or it may be in terms of self-reference. It involves the contact between the subject and object. And could it be a fundamental attribute of all the matter? If so, consciousness may be an attribute that may be explicitly unfolded as seen in the life forms or, in the form of implicate order that remains unexpressed in all matter!

CONSCIOUSNESS IS PRIMORDIAL

Centres in brain of origin of consciousness are well located. Its bio-physics is still obscure. All living forms including plants have an electro-magnetic field is certain. But, consciousness seems to be a quantum electro-dynamic field. Applied to human brain, it leads to the possibility of infinite number of quantum fields in the process of being conscious. Thus, there is infinite degree of freedom to consciousness; and, activity in the brain would be through the interplay of energy fields. There is conclusive evidence about the occurrence of quantum events in botanical and zoological disciplines. Plants synthesize carbohydrates with photosynthesis. Retina produces rhodopsin that stimulates photoreceptors with sun light.

So, philosophically, consciousness is primordial: Entire Cosmos manifests in various forms as derived from universal intelligence. That is ultimate reality. An individual is so connected to universal intelligence—cosmic consciousness and, is an integral part of That. Thou art That, an axiomatic Vedantic saying is so arrived at.

Implicate order that is fundamentally intrinsic to cosmic functioning may not be a physical form of God; nobody has been face to face with such a Reality. Evidence abounds that there is inexhaustible energy in the Universe; even within sub-atomic particles. There is some evidence that consciousness in its pristine pure form is also an energy field (*vide infra*). The horizons of physics of consciousness have widened following creation of a virtual Big Bang in 2012 and, its computer simulation in 2015. This we shall discuss later.

Meditation leads to elimination of ego drives, manipulations of the mind and even mind itself. In the state of *Samadhi,* only pristine pure and sublime consciousness prevails. That instantaneously unites to the source; as a drop of water can merge into sea. This is not only esoteric philosophy: it seems to be a real happening in trance state.

ALTERED STATE OF CONSCIOUSNESS

Meditation brings about a change of personality in several different ways; Dialectic thinking, active mentation, abundance of interests and distinctive individuality are the factors that flower but an experience that "I am the doer", persists.

Progressing further consciousness retains only impressions of facts without their psychological associations. There is modification in the mind so that experience is accepted as it is—without any manipulation. There is an experience of occasional surfacing of the mind having thought modification. There remain variable interpretations due to the mind alternating between verbal and conceptual thinking. An ennobling experience begins when thought modification is non-existent—This state is attained when perception is clear. Subjective projections by the mind are dropped. There is a focus that centres around a thought seed. It may be a *mantra* or a creative visualization of a symbol. When the very nucleus of identity is destroyed, there is a complete cessation of all reactive tendencies. It is an experience in which there is not even a seed of any thought. Ultimately one arrives at the state of meditation that is an end in itself; not a means for the fulfilment of some motive. There is pure and holistic awareness. It is a spiritual experience like benediction. There is infinity of wisdom and the psychological becoming through the functional activities of three *gunas* (all the defenses of ego) come to an end (so there is complete dissolution of ego). There is only That Alone—*Kaivalya.* The consciousness has regained its pristine, pure originality.

What is said is just an elegant description of the process of progression of personality of a meditator over a period of time. It may take long time or, to the gifted, in few sessions only. Therefore, it is useful to begin with simplicity. One may begin by considering meditation as simply an altered state of consciousness. Personal awareness persists to a varying extent till the experience progresses to the state of *Samadhi*. Only to a privileged few this happens instantaneously; most need to practice and enhance the experience of trance to deeper state.

So, it is relevant to discuss more about the nature of consciousness.

Simply stated, to be aware is to be conscious. Awareness may be perceptual of the external world, or it may be self-awareness. Various states of consciousness, familiar to all, may be said to be, awake, sleep, and dreaming. However, unfamiliar to most, there are altogether seven states of consciousness. They are experienced during meditation. They are demarcated so as to be described differently. But one can flow or glide into a different arena as one can go from one geographically demarcated area to other. Thus, there is continuation between all the seven states. Self-awareness persists; with a difference until the Seventh State is reached as *Samadhi*. This will be seen later.

SEVEN STATES OF CONSCIOUSNESS

Awake, Sleep and Dream are familiar to all. During the experience, awareness that "I am there" persists. *Raj Yoga* practice brings about an experience of further states, viz.

Turya

The state of *Turya,* Fourth state is distinctively different. It is tranquil settlement in the state of liberation from action as the doer and transcends to the state of witness. *Turya* has no parts, soundless, the incomprehensible, extends beyond the senses, ultimately may transform to the cessation of all phenomena around oneself. It is all blissful state of joy. The subject—meditator—and the object that is meditated upon, becomes one. The meditator has thus a non dual experience. He merges himself into cosmic consciousness.

The narration of esoteric experiential states, Fourth to Seventh, differs from *Pandit* to *Pandit*. However, to experience any of the states of consciousness is the fundamental attribute of all human beings and, is not culturally restricted or conditioned. When poorly understood, one may call them the varieties of religious experiences. During the experience of Fifth state, the meditator has "out of body" experience and, the Sixth state is where the meditator dwells "without knot", liberated and without ideation. Having stayed in the Sixth state, the meditator gracefully transcends to the Seventh state. That is enlightenment. *Seventh state is Samadhi.* Here the meditation is an end in itself. There is pure and holistic awareness. It is a spiritual experience like benediction. Psychological becoming through the functional activities of mind comes to an end, so there is complete dissolution of ego. Consciousness has regained its pristine, pure originality.

While mystical experience of meditation can occur naturally, certain religious traditions like Hindu rituals, Buddhist tradition of *Vajrayana* practices, Islamic Sufi dance, and Christian prayers can systematically cultivate them. These intuitive connection remains only a glimpse for most of us, because, caught as we are in the cross traffic of the profit and loss in our worldly trade accounts, we are immediately drawn away from this almost 'other worldly' experience; only to remember it as some precious moments. The memory of the precious moments can and do turn into "ever present now". For this to happen repeatedly, we have the doorway open all the time through regular practice of daily meditation.

All kind of meditative practices begin with the Fourth State of consciousness. The process is facilitated by what we have discussed earlier. As the process goes forward, within a few minutes there is onset of Fourth State of consciousness.

Characteristics of Turya

The characteristics of this state are that the mind is quiet, calm and peaceful. A general sense of well-being prevails. The person is awake but the state is more like sleep than awake. It is a state of alert restfulness. In this state there is focalization on the subject, be it an image or a *mantra* and, the marginal inputs fade. The focal point becomes symbolic, i.e. it gathers content that goes on expanding in its abstract meaning. There is attention on the focalized idea but it is not accompanied by any kind of tension. There may be distraction by the surroundings but there is no disturbance. There is choiceless extensive awareness but it is not exclusive of any thing in particular. Surreal metaphors translate into real.

The subjective time moves slowly and an hour may appear to have been only a few minutes. But, if so programmed, the time shall pass very slowly. Or, the time may so undulate that the distinction between the past, present and future is lost. There is shift of space location and one can experience oneself at several different locations in space. This is trance. It may be mild, moderate and intense in depth. And in the state of trance, one may experience the space-time dimension to shift. It is possible to regress in time and be at places at times in the past, that may have been forgotten. There can be time progression too.

PHYSIOLOGICAL CHANGES

The state has been studied extensively physiologically. Initially the pulse rate and the blood pressure rise; but soon go below the resting levels. The respiratory rate rises first but soon falls below the resting level and, as the trance progresses, it may be accompanied by small periods of apnea. The metabolic rate falls steeply and it may fall below the level of sleep. The peripheral flow of blood increases and the body and the face may be flushed.

Plasma cortisol levels decline. There is increased coherence of functions of both the hemispheres of the brain. In the electroencephalogram there is preponderance of alpha waves. There is increase of the galvanic skin resistance.

PSYCHOLOGICAL CHANGES

There are lasting psychological benefits. Overall the stress levels decline. There are better interpersonal relationships. There is realistic goal setting and achievement. There is increase in productivity and creativity. Probably the most important outcome of the process is clarity of perception and the generation of intuitive insight. Creativity takes a quantum jump.

Meditative states of consciousness clarify perception. In every-day living, one is led to several fallacies about perception. Before they become diseases of mind, they persist and perpetuate themselves as neurotic compensation, thus acting as coping mechanisms. As seen earlier, mind is a mirror that has a tendency to gather dust through stress and strife. Better still, the dust should not generate and, if there is any, it must constantly be wiped out. Meditation is the remedy. There is problem of time, the problem of space, the problem of relationships—a multitude of problems are there. *Raj Yoga* is the way of resolving all these problems not separately, but totally.

MEDITATION AND THE MIND

What happens to the mind following the practice of meditation is a transformation. There is awakening of intelligence so that the ground from where the intellect functions—from basal brain to frontal cortex—shifts to prefrontal cortex. Intelligence undergoes a multifold transformation to unfold and expand spirituality. In this profound state of awareness, one is a participant and a witness too. On the way further, the participant and the witness both cease to be. Observer and observed merge; to disappear altogether. This is self-actualization or the peak experience. It is a state of self-realization in the timeless moment!

There is a clear understanding about the perception of time being dependent on the moment of consciousness. While the past and future turn out to be memory and its projections, the ever present *now* becomes the focus: that is mindfulness. Since consciousness itself is modulated, the experience of *now* also subjects itself to a change. Time dilatation and constriction as well as stoppage of time are the natural outcome.

Anatomy of Consciousness

Anatomy of Consciousness and its physiological basis are deciphered scientifically, to an extent. Consciousness seems to be more than a mere function of brain during the meditative state. We have identified the reticular formation in the mid-brain extending down to medulla oblongata as the seat of consciousness. Firing of the cells from the cells located in this region upwards to the cerebrum causes the subject to be conscious. However, such an activity does not happen in isolation and the simultaneous firing of neurons from various locations create a single idea. This may be generating a physical field, like electro-magnetic field. This field may expand as to generate a charismatic aura.

There are some questions about consciousness that cannot be answered. They are important to wonder and ponder. What happens to consciousness at death? Does it reincarnate? If yes, how? What about the consciousness of brain dead person? And finally, what about consciousness of cells in a lab? One can only philosophies.

CONCLUSION ABOUT THE MEDITATIVE PROCESS

In the ultimate state of meditation, there happens a union with the Cosmic Consciousness and duality between the observer and observed disappears. Obviously there is no scope for a vitiated perception and, incorrect action arising from there.

However, beginners wonder as to how to meditate. "How to do" is a basic question that can be addressed now.

Chapter 4

Initial Steps to Transformation of Consciousness

Meditation is a state of freedom; there is no need to be structured by any format. Whatever construct is given is for narration. There can be choice to begin from any step. It is to be reiterated again and again: meditation happens spontaneously to a few enlightened souls like Socrates, Ramakrishana Paramhansa and Krishnamurthi. It can be learnt as taught by Vivekananda and many others that followed. Meditation may just *happen* to a few esoteric, privileged few; most of us will have to learn it. One can sit down and begin with well charted steps to begin with. Transformation of consciousness progresses for sure, since it is a fundamental attribute of all mankind to be pristine pure. So, let us enumerate some initial steps.

POSITION OF COMFORT

The meditative posture should be a position of comfort. For the initial stages especially at a young age, the recommended posture is *Padmasana*. If this causes discomfort, one may begin with *Ardha Padmasana*. These postures stretch the muscles and, the nerves along with them. Therefore, a situation of alert wakefulness is obtained right from the beginning. However a particular posture is not an imperative must. A sick person can meditate even lying down in the bed.

Meditative process involves enlargement of electro-magnetic field of the persona. It is, therefore, important to sit/relax in such a way that body should not be in contact with a good conductor of electricity.

Addition of some *Hatha Yoga* practices, performing some postures before or after the meditative practice is beneficial. A composite single posture, like *Surya Namaskara*, involves the entire body and has a symbolic meditative meaning to it. However, individual sensibilities should prevail. There are no cultural boundaries, for instance Kathryn Rossi meditates upon *Hanuman* and chooses to combine meditative practices with *Hatha Yoga* practices in the end.

PRANAYAMA

Pranayama is wrongly translated as breathing exercises. It is a special technique for control of breathing. Techniques abound in several distinct forms; one may begin with simple inhalation and exhalation with the time duration as 1 to 2. Soon, one should graduate to be able to withhold the breath with the gap so as to perform, *Anuloma Viloma Pranayama*. This has inhalation retention and exhalation ratio as 1:4:2. The normal breathing rate is around 18 per minute. With a regular practice, this may come down to 10 or 12. When breathing slows down a further extension of retention after exhalation may be added. It is hypothesized that retention of the breath will increase carbon dioxide levels in the body. Carbon dioxide levels around five per cent are conducive to the growth of stem cells spread all over the body. The respiratory centre is located in medulla oblongata. The neurons responsible for regulation of consciousness are spread as substantia nigra from medulla oblongata up to pons. Differential firing of respiratory centre may be effective in generating a different state of consciousness.

Several thousands of thoughts and ideas cross the mind during the course of a single day. Unfinished agenda, as of a single day or since any time past, surface in dreams. It may appear that to give up the thought processing by the mind is almost impossible. An attempt to push away one idea may bring to surface several other thoughts. Even a slight opening in the window of the unconscious mind will bring several bizarre ideas. If any of this idea dominates, the meditation will not progress. A simple technique is to avoid all ideas as unwelcome guests; not to fight with them, nor to entertain them.

Within a few minutes only there is a transgression to trance. However, about 2 per cent of people fail to experience the Fourth State. Regulation of breath in a cyclic pattern is a great facilitation.

As the breathing changes to a different mode and yet, in ordinary conscious state of awareness, there is automatic attention on the breath. There is a start to the meditative process without a clear demarcation; though, "I have changed to a different mode of breathing" is noted. The subjective element, I, persists in the following stages up to a point when duality disappears; that we will see later.

However the process has begun.

PARADIGM SHIFT IN CONSCIOUSNESS

Meditation occurs only through a paradigm shift in consciousness. The shift may begin with *pranayama,* since during the practice, the attention is drawn to the regulation of breath. During this state of attention, focalization may occur to breathing itself. An experience of a transformation begins. For a moment, while regulating breath, a moment arrives when the mind stops thinking. This may only be a momentary pause. But, it amounts to discovery of a new domain in consciousness. One such feeling of "*Aha!*"; *Now I know! Now I know what it is!* Subsequently, forceful denial to thought processes disappears by itself; *Aha* experience predominates and, takes precedence to wean away from all random ideas. *Pratyahar* may simply prevail as the observation of watching what is happening only now: At any moment it is only breathing that keeps on happening; every other activity in the mind is cast away.

A PAUSE

While the attention is focused on the regulation of the breath, there is an automatic change of the track. It causes transformation of consciousness from ordinary awake state to the *Fourth* state. Neuroscience of this transformation is still under study. It is certain that though it appears like a mechanical change of track by a fast moving train, it is much more different. Functioning of the neuronal connections in the brain and the transmission of information at the synapses is far more intricate. It involves the secretion of molecular biological substances at synaptic junctions. Further, quantum phenomena seem to occur in the process of information transfer. Quantum tunnelling, (*vide infra*), whereby the information is transferred between two unconnected objects, is most likely to be happening at the neuronal junctions. This transfer that may occur at the speed of light (this is the highest speed that any particle can travel. There is a hypothesis that there are particles named as tachyons that travel faster) will still involve some minimal time duration for a fraction of a nano second. That translates as a pause.

The stipulated pause in neuronal transmission seems to be as much important as a pause between two different activities in everyday life. A pause is refreshing and the subsequent restart to a different activity is enjoyable. Transformation to the *turya* state is probably facilitated on account of the quantum phenomena at the synapses.

There are forms of meditation that focus on only breath. Focalization means exclusion of other objects. Thus, *pranayama* can itself become a focal point for meditation.

MINDFULNESS MEDITATION

It is appropriate to discuss here techniques that dwell on breathing primarily, and progress therefrom. Mindfulness, a Buddhist meditation technique is one such refined technique. Here, one simply dwells on the present moment; to the total exclusion of the past and future. Perception of the breathing is to focus on ones own present moment. Obviously, meditating on the breath, one remains in present moment. That is mindfulness of "Now"! Past is absolute; future remains uncertain. This technique is training to live at the present moment. Mindfulness has been tested scientifically; is simple to start practice. It is one of the most popular currency as of now in the West. Matthew Ricard turned a monk after his doctorate from Pasteur University, France. He spent 20 + years in Himalayas and in Buddhist monasteries. He lived for sometime in proximity to the Dalai Lama. He conducted several investigations on mindfulness and is now teaching courses worldwide.

This technique can progress to *Vipassana*.

Vipassana

Vipassana is a word in Pali language. It is derived from Sanskrit. It translates as special perception; that is to see reality as it is. To see reality as it is would only be right perception. Right perception is the right action.

There are several steps to progress in *Vipassana*. The first step is to observe the ever present happening to a human being;

that is breathing. *Vipassana* focuses on observation of inhalation and exhalation process to begin with. This is akin to mindfulness meditation. While doing so, the technique is to avoid all ideas as unwelcome guests; not to fight with them, nor to entertain them. Simply observation of breathing—*Anapana Sati*—causes automatic slowing down of thought processes. (*Sati*, again a word in Pali, means mindfulness). And, one can transcend to other steps of focalization from there.

Anapana Sati

This technique is to focus on breathing. There is moment to moment awareness of one's own breathing. Here one has to observe natural breath that goes in and comes out: Just no other thoughts, no other objects. Be aware in an effortless, choiceless passive manner. If the mind wavers on any count, it has to be brought back to observation of breathing. This happens quietly with passive submissiveness.

Breathing is a vital process, it occurs spontaneously. Hence, it is easy and handy technique. Breathing is the carrier of emotions. Breathing changes with different emotions and perversions. With anger and hatred breathing becomes fast. With jealousy, it becomes irregular. With a sense of love and compassion pervading not only for the sentient beings but, for the environment in its entirety, it becomes slow and rhythmic. So, for a practitioner of *anapana sati*, breath becomes a feedback.

Further Progress in Vipassana

Vipassana meditation can progress to a reflection on *kayanupassana* (observation of the parts of the body and their functions). Observation on the flow of the breath now transgresses to the memory of the body. Various parts and organs are the objects of contemplation. Progressing further,

Vedanaanupassana observes the flow of the emotions and feelings. This helps in development of a subtle sharp mind without being carried away by sentiments. So, we are still dealing with mind and attempting to delete its manipulations. *Chitta- anupassana* passively reflects on the contents of the mind and, that will facilitate critical thinking. *Dhammanupassyana*, a contemplation on the philosophical aspects of spiritual experience like nature, inherent quality in various manifestations thereof, nature of void, merit, and *samadhi* is the final stage of *vipassanna* meditation.

It may appear that *Vipassana* may probably be the best choice: additionally it relates to somewhat to mindfulness meditation that has scientific validation. However, there are several alternate beautiful panoramic vistas beyond. Classically, *Vipassana* entails a structured initiation. It is required for the initiate to isolate for 7-10 days in a sanctuary. While other aspirants are around, there is no communication between them. One is required to attend/listen to lectures or video cassettes. This may not suit to some with different sensibilities. Those who have undergone the initiation; revel in its praise. For others who may find it hard to undergo such hard *tapa* there are several alternatives that we shall explore as we progress along the royal road charted by Patanjali.

Chapter 5

Neuroscience of Meditation

We have axiomatically accepted that there is a transformation of mind and consciousness through the process of trance. We should now explore what is the established science as well as metaphysics. That will reaffirm the relevance of meditative practices in everyday life.

We have two distinctively opposite paradigms concerning the nature of consciousness. Biologists and neuroscientist will define it as an epiphenomenon arising autonomously from brain. It arises with the development of brain—there is evidence that it arises as soon as there is elementary development of brain in embryo—and dies with it. This will not explain, even with complex molecular biology of information substances, the behaviour of cells in and outside living systems. Cells communicate at near and far distances, multiply with harmony and as per the dictates of morphogenetic fields. They undergo mass death—apoptosis when competition to survive is too much. And, there is a protein called ubiquitin that has come to be known as the "Kiss of Death—since that eliminates any cell when it comes in contact with. That sets the cycle of regeneration and rejuvenation in motion."

In spite of its limitations, this paradigm is the currency with medical science today. A brain dead person is declared virtually dead since he cannot regain consciousness.

There is alternate mode in total contradiction to the above.

Consciousness came first, even before Big Bang. Or may be the first natural phenomenon after Big Bang. Indian Classical concept based on Vedantic philosophy epitomizes consciousness as primordial. It is all abounding, all pervading and indestructible energy. It is already there when the fertilization occurs and, it persists even after death. So that it may reincarnate in another form. The entire cosmos is primarily filled with cosmic intelligence—cosmic consciousness—and, all the matter, living and non-living, are just the "concretization" form of it. A living system is just like a pot of water that is filled with the water of sea of cosmic intelligence. Or it is like a radio set that receives the signals; and, it may receive and transmit information as does an internet connected computer. The computer or radio may become dysfunctional; but super computer that makes the Universe whirl around, is not affected.

Present day practices in most disciplines demand a proof with evidence. Highly sophisticated tools are now available to science in 21st Century provided for investigations. The transforming power of Yoga and meditation to the consciousness and, their application in life must be supported by evidence. This should come not only from the wisdom of sages with the help of Vedic texts and, exposure to different meditative practices. But there should also be validation with peer reviewed and validated science. We now provide objective evidence for the neural and biological basis for meditation. The evidence relies only on published data. The disciplines covered are molecular biology, medicine, gene expression studies and quantum physics including metaphysics. It will establish meditation as the ground of creativity, happiness, and health, An understanding of hypnotherapy, may be with a different name—*Yoga nidra*—will remove bias against it; and, will favour its inclusion as one of the facet of *Raj Yoga.*

Maharshi Mahesh Yogi established Maharshi European Research University in Switzerland. This University has published voluminous research to prove the physiological basis of meditative states. The research got additional validation by the work of Herbert Benson. He went to Dharmashala, India to study on the long time Buddhists meditators. In contrast to life time work of Hans Selye that is well recognized as "Stress Response", this came to be known as Relaxation Response.

Meditation brings about a transformation of consciousness. In the process, there is expansion of consciousness too. Enumerated as eight empowerments—*Vibhuti*—Patanjali called this extension as *Siddhies.* He named them as micro-sensing, macro-sensing, levitation, charisma (increase in the hallow effect), (enumerated in Sanskrit respectively as; *anima, mahima,* (a physical expansion of electro-magnetic field or simply a condensation of large mass) *laghima, garima, prapti, prakamya, isita and vashita;* we shall explore the understanding about them later). All that are a *happening*, may be occult and unexplainable. It is not to be sought; it happened and, had to be ignored. Seeking and running after *Siddhies* will waver and deviate the practitioner from the path. However, *Siddhies* do come to happen and, need to be explained as to how do the accomplishments occur. Whatever opinion one may subscribe to about the nature of consciousness, there is abundant evidence that it is not confined to brain alone.

Philosophy is the mother of all science. What is a hypothesis today may come to be proven science some day.

Some phenomena happen; when they are not common and unexplainable by the reason as it prevails today, we call it occult. Science of tomorrow will provide the rationale of paranormal occurrences as of today. The present age has the capability to explain all that truly is happening and, discard fraud and magic. Science may not explain all of the Nature; but it certainly accepts the veracity of the verifiability of the unexplained phenomena. Expansion of consciousness is one such happening that occurs in trance state and its plausible explanations are likely through physics and metaphysics

Raj Yoga is practiced by different names. The techniques vary. Academic Western researchers club them to gather as mind-body approaches. Various forms of meditation including repetitive prayer, different schools of *Yoga, tai chi and Qi Gong* (Chinese practices that includes martial arts too), breathing exercises, progressive muscle relaxation, biofeedback and guided imagery bring about a physiological change that is named as relaxation response. In general, various forms of meditation up regulates parasympathetic system. However, it is more than relaxation, concentration, contemplation or posturing as we will see later.

Let us study the science in easily palatable fashion.

GENE EXPRESSION

A pioneering study by Richard Davidson at Wisconsin University and subsequently by others, reported evidence of specific gene expression changes in the body following a period of mindfulness meditation. There was alterations in gene expression in subjects practicing with mindfulness meditation. There is a down-regulation of genes—decreasing in the activity—that have been implicated in stress. Gene expression studies are sophisticated and highly expensive. Scientific studies require quantification for comparison between groups. Thus the research is fastidious. Yet, it is now established that relaxation response elicitation results in differential gene expression characteristic of regeneration and rejuvenation. Studies in *Raj Yoga* and *vajrayana* meditation are distinctively advanced different techniques that end in elimination of mind at the stage of *Samadhi* and *sunyata* respectively. Further research in these areas promise more illuminating results.

However, it is established that there is a definitive distinct change in personality that amounts to transformation of consciousness. Physiologically, relaxation response is characterized by decreased oxygen consumption, increase in exhaled nitric oxide, reduction in levels of stress hormones and over all sense of well-being and happiness. We study some elementary data about physiology.

MOLECULAR BIOLOGY

We have known hormones to be the principal molecules regulating body functions till late 20th century. Now, we know that a single cell can secretes about 150 cytokines—molecular biological substances that have different functions. New age science of bioinformatics provides us the information about transmission cross talk between the molecules without actually performing experiments in laboratory. Meditative process permeates to each and every cell in the body (Fig. 5.1). Molecular biological process is in the following manner. There are ideas and thoughts. There are emotions. Thoughts are in the form of suprathalamic stimuli that are conveyed in the form electrical impulses to the centres lower down. There may as well be another mode of transport in the form of molecular substances secreted by the brain cells at hypothalamus, limbic system and several other areas all over the body. Our understanding of these kinds of interplay between the electrical impulses, secretion of neurotransmitters, neurohormones, neuropeptides and several other molecules like endorphins, opiates, valium and others are in pipeline of discovery. Candace Pert initially has established a link between emotions and their molecular equivalence. The molecules of emotions are floating as particles in the blood stream and, also in extra cellular fluid. Putting it other way, cerebral stimuli in the form of thoughts and emotions have their molecular equivalents.

We just review only a few that meditation modulates.

ENDORPHINS

Endorphins are neuro-hormone secreted by brain, other parts of central nervous system and pituitary gland. Discovered by Candace Pert, it established an astonishing fact that brain is the largest endocrine gland! It leads to the validation of the hypothesis that there indeed are molecules of emotions! We have seen that events and experiences that are heavily loaded with emotional content such as wonder, awe, astonishment, anger and ecstasy get stored as long term memory. This has a molecular basis; relieving the event may be considered as recreating the molecular structure that may have been at the actual time of happening. Physiologically this has come to be known as a state dependent memory.

Literally endorphins mean a morphia like substance secreted by the body itself. Their secretion in the body is primarily as pain relieving agents. But like morphia, they have additional effects such as the experience of euphoria. The joy happiness and ecstasy, *Aha* and *Ananda* as commonly experienced during and after meditation may be attributed to endorphin and other molecules that are proven to be associated with altered states of consciousness.

Some find it addictive too; this may be attributed to its similarity with morphine. Meditation is a mental process to enhance productivity, creativity and peace. A duration of 20 minutes in the morning and evening should suffice towards this goal. Vinoba Bhave a lesser known master exponent of *Raj Yoga* admonished his Ashramites against prolonged duration of practice.

DOPAMINE

Dopamine is a neurohormone. It is responsible for the awake state. It can enhance the joy of finding—the "eureka!" It is also released by the hypothalamus. It has many functions in behaviour and cognition such as voluntary movements, motivation, punishment and reward and prolactin production inhibition. It is rated to play a role in pain processing in multiple levels of the central nervous system. Dopamine increases general arousal and goal directed behaviour and, decreases latent inhibition; all three effects increase the creative drive of idea generation. (See Fig. 5.2)

Dopamine is produced in several areas of the brain including the hypothalamus. Dopamine has many functions in the brain, including important roles in behaviour and cognition, voluntary movement, motivation, punishment and reward, sleep, mood, attention, working memory, and learning. Dopamine has a role in pain processing at multiple levels of the central nervous system. It increases the creative drive of idea generation.

MELATONIN

Melatonin is secreted into the blood by the *pineal gland* in the brain. It is best secreted in darkness. It may also be produced by a variety of peripheral cells such as *bone marrow cells*, lymphocytes, and *epithelial cells* (see Fig. 5.3).

Melatonin is a *geroprotector*. Melatonin receptors appear to be important in mechanisms of learning and memory such as *long-term potentiation* (LTP). In *perimenopausal* women it produces an improvement in thyroid function and *gonadotropin* levels, as well as restoring fertility and menstruation and preventing the depression associated with the menopause. Melatonin is an effective *preventive treatment* for *migraine* and, since it ameliorates circadian misalignment, it is the only drug for jet lag after travel. It is an anti-oxidant and suppressant of tumour development. Melatonin acts as a mild hypnotic. Melatonin is effective in treating depression and *seasonal affective disorder.*

A study at M.S. University, Vadodara, has proved that there is a pulsatile production of melatonin under/after hypnosis. However, the long term practitioners of meditation have higher levels of melatonin. This will explain regeneration and rejuvenation since melatonin has even anti aging properties. A clear message has already emerged from the results: there is a pulsatile production of melatonin under/after hypnosis. Long time practioners of meditation, on the other hand, have a persistent higher normal level of melatonin. This will explain several regenerative and rejuvenating outcomes following hypnotherapy as well as wellness of the meditators.

OXYTOCIN

Oxytocin causes the feeling of being safe and bonded in social situations. It acts as a *neuro-modulator* in the *brain*. In *lactating* mothers it causes flow of milk. It is important for *cervical dilation* before birth and causes contractions during the second and third stages of *labor*. This explains the facilitation of labor with hypnosis. There is correlation of oxytocin with human bonding; increase in trust, and decrease in fear are attributed to the hormone. Certain learning and memory functions are impaired by centrally administered oxytocin. Oxytocin is involved in the initiation of maternal behaviour. Oxytocin inhibits the development of tolerance to various addictive drugs (*opiates, cocaine, alcohol*) and reduces *withdrawal* symptoms. This explains the application of meditation for de-addiction. Oxytocin also modulates *inflammation* and is thus involved in wound healing.

CORTISONE

Cortisone is primarily a stress hormone. It has wide ranging effects with receptors all over the body; most predominant in mesenchymal tissues. It suppresses immunity, inflammation and, causes swelling of the tissues. It has psychotrophic effects too. There is reduction in the excessive release of this hormone through meditation.

Evidence as provided so far does confirm that mind-body is a single entity. Each affects the other. In this discussion, consciousness is absent, since biological sciences equate ordinary awake state as consciousness. This has come to pass because in the West, study of biochemical interactions became the prevailing paradigm to explain cellular functions and disease progression.

Pharmaceutical industry subsequently became very successful in using this model in developing a series of effective drugs. That has transformed medicine into a huge business. During the 20th century medical treatments became largely based on drug therapies. Pharmaceutical manufacturers have come to be a dominant influence in medicine. Now supremacy of the biochemical paradigm and pharmaceutical influences have caused almost all research in medicine to be directed toward understanding the chemistry of the body and, the effects that drugs have on altering that chemistry. Consciousness does not figure in this paradigm except in psychiatry. And, psychiatrists are still baffled about consciousness. There are indications that psychiatry has overlooked major problems, if not a whole dimension. Many biological questions cannot be answered with biochemical explanations alone such as the role of endogenously created electro-magnetic fields and electrical currents in the body. Some of the questions remain unanswered, Biochemical explanations alone fail to explain the role of electricity in cellular regulation. It is plausible that the cells of the body possess *electrical mechanisms* and use electricity to regulate and control the transduction of chemical energy and other life processes.

Thus we arrive at a bifurcation point for further scientific explorations of consciousness. It postulates a further extension of dimension to consciousness that it is energy. And, energy does influence matter. Energy cannot be destroyed; it only gets transformed to a different mode. That takes us to hard core science of physics.

ELECTRO-MAGNETIC FIELDS

Electromagnetic fields have information and communication roles. They are employed by living organisms as information conveyors from the environment to the living systems, within the organism and among organisms. They are involved in life's vital processes. They facilitate pattern formation in the organization (morphogenetic fields) and control growth. So, living organisms possess the ability to utilize electro-magnetic fields and electricity. There must be physical structures within the cells that facilitate the sensing, transducing, storing and transmitting of this form of energy (Fig. 5.4). Demonstration of electro-magnetic field between two hands is diploid in induction of hypnosis for clinical applications.

Application in Medicine

Evidence is just emerging that hypnotherapy can help cure/ relieve psychological problems. On the other hand, British Medical Association and American Medical Association have listed several conditions like that can be helped with strategic hypnotherapy that is applied in the state of *turya.* They include migraine, irritable bowel syndrome and ulcerative colitis. Based on the axiomatic proposition that mind body interaction influences each other, arthritis, allergies of various kinds, asthma, life style diseases such as hypertension, diabetes, coronary artery disease, chronic constipation, menopausal syndrome, menstrual discomfort (dysmenorrhoea), fibromyalgia, depression and anxiety. The list covers about 100 conditions that include quitting the smoking habit and substance abuse. Most of the skin conditions respond, at times instantaneously. Even life threatening disease such as pemphigus do get cured! Suffice it to say that there is mind-body continuum and most psychosomatic diseases, terminal cancer related pain and auto-immune diseases such as multiple sclerosis, rheumatoid arthritis and others can be alleviated.

A medical doctor, Swami Satyananda Saraswati established Bihar School of Yoga. Meditation technique by this school has been named as *Yoga nidra.* It almost corresponds with self-hypnosis (Table 5.1).

BRAIN MAPPING AND IMAGING

The clinical evidence is buttressed by neuroimaging with MRI, and fMRI that provides data regarding regional cerebral blood flow. MEG (magnetoencephalography) and improved EEG (electroenphalography) allow detailed studies in understanding the effect of meditation on neural behaviour. A study on Buddhist lamas in the year 2000 proved that higher meditative states are no more hallucinations. They are actual neurobiological phenomena.

MRI Changes during Meditation

Various radiological imaging techniques such as single-photon emission computed tomography (SPECT is an imaging technique using *gamma rays*), positron emission tomography (PET is a nuclear medicine functional imaging technique that is used to observe metabolic processes in brain)

Table 5.1 : Hypnosis *Versus* Meditation

	Hypnosis	*Meditation*
1.	Scientific and therapeutic	Spiritual
2.	Subject of scientific scrutiny	Philosophical
3.	Studied scientifically since last two centuries	Spiritual experience since ages
4.	Fertile ground for research; difficult to quantify the experience	Difficult to quantify
5.	Any one can learn	A moral and ethical code of living is a prerequisite before initiation; esoteric
6.	Goal oriented	There are many kinds of Samadhi: goal oriented; goalless; and Nameless experience
7.	Relaxation and deep breathing are utilized as induction tools	Stillness of body and mind is essential; esoteric breathing exercises, pranayam, facilitate the experience
8.	Utilized for therapeutic healing and for personality development	Health giving, disease preventing and helps spiritual growth
9.	Self hypnosis is easy to learn and practice and can be taught individually and in group by academicians	Requires a guru. Difficult to find a bonafide guru
10.	Archetypal symbols and meaningful images may be utilized	Focalization on a form of sound, mantra or visual symbol of a deity
11.	Insight generation and creativity is a step by step process	It is a pathless land where there is no destination, no goal. Enlightenment "happens"
12.	Guided hypnosis is unlikely to do any harm	Meditation has driven people crazy when not practiced under the supervision of a guru or a guide
13.	Freedom from affliction by hypnotherapy	Attainment of kaivalya – Journey alone to Alone

and functional magnetic resonance imaging or fMRI (fMRI is a procedure that measures brain activity by detecting changes associated with blood flow), allow examination of changes in activation of the brain. Several studies showed that:

- The parietal lobe of the brain is thought to be responsible for giving us a sense of our orientation in time and space. By blocking all sensory and cognitive input into this area, meditation results in the sense of no space and no time.
- Prefrontal lobe area is well developed only in humans. High cognitive capacity of judgment, intuitive memory, ability to perform complex tasks with tactfulness along with rational evolved behaviour and social etiquette are the functions of this area. During meditation, blood flow increases in this area.
- fMRI studies literally unfolded the whole circuitry involved in meditation process and demonstrated a significant increase in signals in prefrontal and parietal cortices during meditation.
- Neural structures involved in attention and control of autonomic nervous system are activated.

Most types of meditation, which involve an initial focusing of *attention*, are associated with increased regional blood flow or glucose metabolism in the prefrontal areas that are important in selection of a mental task. The radiological imaging established the proofs that:

- The frontal lobes, especially the prefrontal regions help to organize, prioritize, plan and focus attention.
- During *visualization* regional blood flow increases in the "visual cortex" and visual association areas in the occipital lobes.
- In *contemplation* of "self" the parietal lobes on both sides are activated.
- Meditation appears to begin by activating prefrontal associated with the will or intent to clear one's mind of

thoughts or to focus on an object.

- There occurs a differentiation in functioning of parietal lobe, There is a decrease in arrival of distracting stimuli, enhancing focus. This results in altered perception of self-experience.
- *Thalamus* filters sensory information before it reaches the cerebral cortex. During meditation it filters sensory inputs to part of the parietal lobe causing a different sense of body awareness. Increased thalamic blood flow implies that there is an active process of filtering and processing of information about the body.
- There is increased activity in the inner aspect of the temporal lobe. That affects functional connections with autonomic nervous system. Thus, integration of autonomic nervous system activity with different parts of brain is increased.

Neuroplasticity: Increase in Connectivity

Recent findings on neuroplasticity showed that brain regions associated with attention and introspection like prefrontal cortex were thicker in meditation practitioners. Prefrontal cortices thickness was most pronounced in participants with long practice. Thus meditation offsets age related cortical thinning.

In summary, it is plausible that almost all meditation practices change the functioning of brain and, promote neuroplasticity. Fundamentally, there has to be an experience of *turya.* There is charisma around the personality that can be explained by expansion of electro-magnetic field around the persona of the meditator. Development of several faculties remains unexplained. This may be happening through phenomena in physics. We shall study them now.

QUANTUM PHYSICS

Classical Newtonian Physics studies materials and, fields around them. Quantum physics takes the consciousness as the determinant phenomenon. This was widely disputed for a long time and discussions still continue since there is still not a comprehensive unified field theory. Equations pertaining to all the four fundamental fields in physics are valid independently of each other. So, let us understand a little about quantum physics that is studied the least in living systems.

Of course, the perception of light by the retina is a quantum event in the form of a photon interacting with the neural tissue of the retina. This may extend to quantum electrodynamics. The entire nervous system functions through the generation and propagation of electrical impulses. The electrical potentials will generate an electro-magnetic field. And the electrical activity occurs at the synapses as well as in the neuronal cells. Though not completely deciphered as yet, the complex actions at the genetic levels, from the arousal of a certain gene to the message transmission and transduction by mRNA may also involve electrical activity. Thus, there is indeed a real possibility about the occurrence of quantum events at various levels from brain to the cell membrane all over the body. This can bring about the play of not only electro-magnetic fields but quantum fields as well.

Quantum Phenomena at Synapses

A nerve cell looks like a tree under the microscope. It has a main trunk, which is axon, and several other branches that are called dendrites. The axon is the main communicating channel but the dendrites also carry the electric impulse to the sites where they may be ending. There is no direct connection of an axon or dendrites to another cell. There is a gap in between. That is called a synapse. We saw interplay of biological molecules at a gross level. It may appear that the information is relayed at a synapse for onward transmission through the release of neuro-transmitter molecules. But the matter can be highly complex. In the actions that come into play at the synapses, it is quite probable that quantum events may occur.

The size of a synaptic junction is about 200 to 400 Angstroms, i.e. very small. When a nerve impulse arrives at the end of an axon, it is in the form of an electric impulse. It causes the release of neurotransmitter substances so as to activate the other cell. The neurotransmitter substances are much smaller in size than the synaptic cleft, yet it may be assumed that they will crawl up to the adjacent cell and incite electric impulse over there. This may indeed be happening but if that was the exclusive way, the function of the nervous system will be very tardy. We see it operating almost in flashes. Therefore, modalities other than the actual contact with a neurotransmitter substance must be occurring. For this kind of speeds, a mere chemical reaction will not suffice. It can be a quantum event involving quantum fields.

Quantum Field

A field is that region in which a force is experienced originating from one source that acts on the other bodies within a particular region. A field is space equipped with potentiality. In quantum field theory, elementary particles are represented as fields.

And, a phenomenon called quantum mechanical tunnelling may occurs in transmission of information between the articles. Quantum mechanical tunnelling is a phenomenon where by an electron pierces through a barrier, alters the electric potential and then causes a cascade of electrons. If such quantum events were to happen, they would create corresponding quantum electrodynamic fields. It can, therefore, be inferred that these spatio-temporal fields of influence are exerted by the mind—psychic processes—on the brain in willed action.

Quantum Consciousness

This brings us to a point where in the consciousness as a perceptual awareness may be different than the *quantum consciousness* at each and every cellular point in the brain and body. This is then the physical location of the consciousness as well as a possible explanation as to how does it occur. It can possibly be said that a unit of consciousness is *single quantum electrodynamic field (QED)*. That would mean that the consciousness is a field that is distinctively different from what we have so far called perceptual awareness.

The idea that we have arrived at is as different as the quantum physics from classical physics. Accepting that there is a physiological basis to awareness being perceived at the cerebral level, we repeat that there is a distinctively different class of consciousness that is in the form of a field. And there are innumerable units of quantum fields at each and every cellular level as well as synapses. This leads to a multiplicity of vast number of fields generated by the quantum events all over the body. Summation of this at the individual level will give a hologram that is individual consciousness.

If the individual holographic unit of quantum consciousness were to merge with such other hologram, it will further constitute larger and larger hologram(s). So a single holographic pattern of collective consciousness of a group and subsequently, that of universal consciousness, should be obvious. The nature of universal consciousness is then, in the form of unbroken wholeness. An individual consciousness is just a fragmented explicit aspect of universal Nature. The explicit order in Nature is unfolded as individual consciousness. But Universal consciousness is enfolded as implicate order in *all that exists in*

Nature; be it apparently inert matter or living biological systems. Two taken together only will make for the whole.

Thus, consciousness in matter in any form can be understood as implicate order. Individual consciousness is only a fragmented actuality. May be through the quantum phenomena, connectivity is reestablished with the integrated wholistic consciousness that pervades the Universe as implicate order. If matter and consciousness could in this way be understood together the way could be opened to comprehend their relationship on the basis of this common ground.

Further Observations in Quantum Physics

The role of the observer in quantum phenomena remains an unresolved enigma. Does quantum physics say goodbye to material reality? This a moot question that leads to uneasy conclusion that reality does not exist when we are not observing it. This is akin to that what Vedanta has been saying for ages! Similarly the implications of observations related to "Entangled Particles" are mind-boggling.

Quantum Tunnelling

We postulated information transduction between two non-contiguous electrically charged poles at synaptical junctions in neuronal junctions. That may be happening through a quantum phenomenon called *quantum tunnelling.* It is a surprising co-incidence that this discovering won Nobel Prize for Josephson. He was one of the foremost practitioner of transcendental meditation! He discovered that a *supercurrent* could tunnel through a barrier. This became known as the Josephson effect and the junction as a Josephson junction.

Now, the gap between two neurons at synaptic junction is very, very small. However, the phenomenon of entangled particles that exchange information even when seperated by a huge distance may also be attributed to *quantum tunnelling*. Thus, Josephson is one of the few scientists to argue that parapsychological phenomena (*telepathy, psychokinesis* and other paranormal themes) may be real discoveries that can be quantum events.

TM movement produced a poster showing Josephson levitating several inches above the floor. A group of physicists interested in investigating psychic occurences emerged as Fysiks Group, the University of California, Berkeley. Leading members included *Fritjof Capra*, *John Clauser*, Philippe Eberhard, *Nick Herbert*, *Jack Sarfatti*, Saul-Paul Sirag, *Henry Stapp*, and *Fred Alan Wolf*. They used ideas from quantum physics, particularly *Bell's theorem* and *quantum entanglement*, to explore issues such as *action at a distance*, *clairvoyance*, *precognition*, *remote viewing* and *psychokinesis*. The hard core physicists are in denial code; yet, the interest persists and would do so, till paranormal occurrences are explained.

Mind-Matter Unification Project at the Cavendish Laboratory considers quantum mechanics as the future science. Quantum entanglement between various fields of consciousness will be one of the manifestations of such organisation.

Summarizing, physics is our model of a perfect science: it has mathematical basis. But, our perfect model is an incomplete model and the part may give a glimpse of the whole; but it cannot substitute for the whole.

Sri Aurobindo said: "The matter shall reveal the face of spirit". The poetical statement was not a mere aesthetic fantasy. *Rishis* are endowed with a special faculty of extraordinary perception through the practice of *Raj Yoga*. We shall examine some of the evidences that point in this direction.

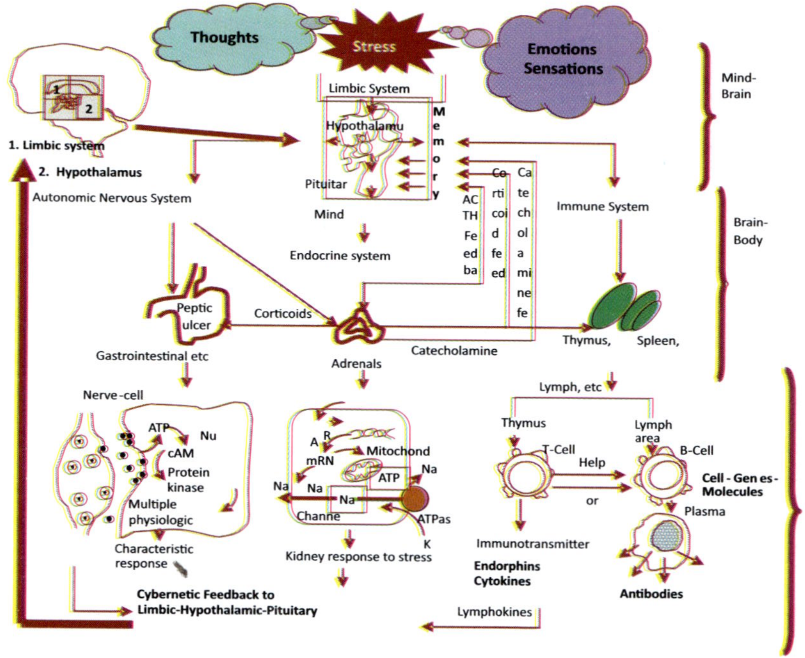

Fig. 5.1: Cybernatic Mind–Body Feed Back to Limbic – Hypothalamic – Pituitary – Cell Receptors Axis

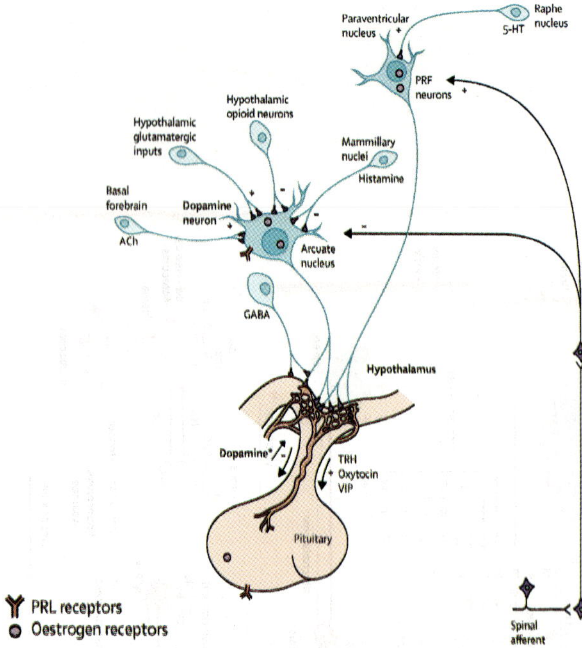

Fig. 5.2: Hypothalamus-pitutary Axis with Dopamine & Oxytocin

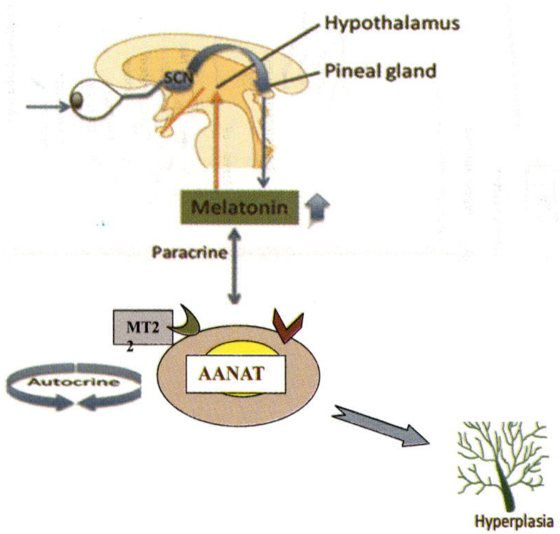

Fig. 5.3: Signalling pathway for Melatonin secretion in dark hours

Fig. 5.4: Electromagnetic field between two hands

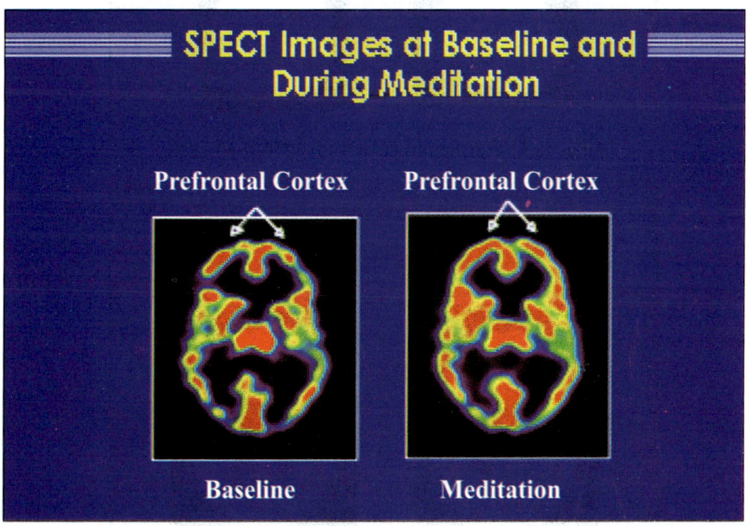

Fig. 5.5: Frontal Lobes

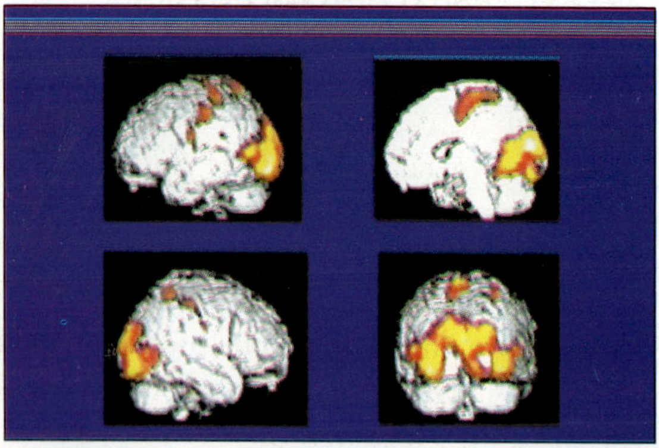

Fig. 5.6: Visual Imagery

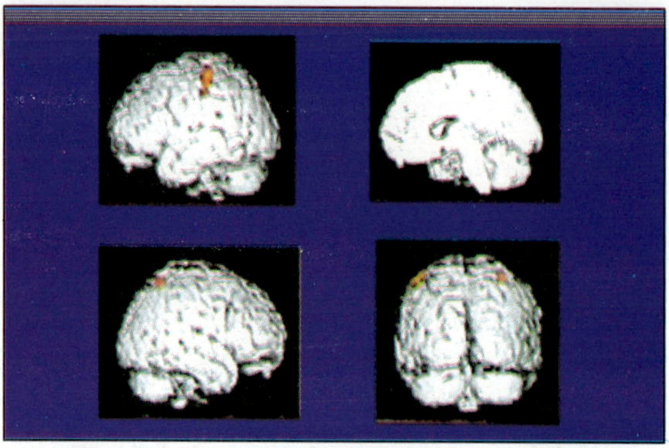

Fig. 5.7: Symbolic representation of Self

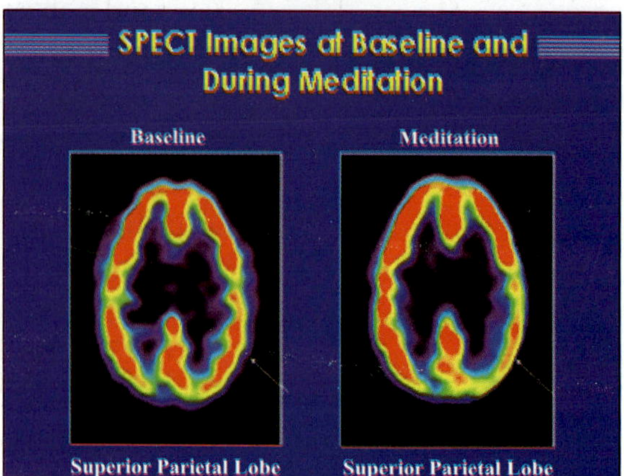

Fig. 5.8: SPECT images

EEG (ELECTROENCEPHALOGRAM) CHANGES

There are four types of waves in EEG: alpha, beta, theta and delta. The meditation brainwave pattern is a combination of alpha and theta. In general amplitude of alpha wave improves with slowing of its frequency. Rhythmic theta waves appear and there is increased synchronization pattern of alpha. Alpha wave pattern is in the 7-14 Hz range and theta is below that. Going into deep relaxation and meditation, one enters the "alpha-theta state" where brain activity slows almost to the point of sleep. This is a state that brings heightened receptivity, connects us to our unconscious mind (that we are ordinarily unconscious of) and, awakens intuition. It can be said that any thought projected in the mind at this level will certainly be manifested in real life. We shall examine this proposition later in greater detail in our discussions on *Dhyana.* Meanwhile, we continue to study certain coincidences that at a first look, may not look significant. However, Nature works in high economic, frugal ways. It does not waste energy. So, let us look at a few such occurrences.

The 8 Hz Frequency Puzzle

Ionosphere is the layer of the earth's atmosphere that contains a high concentration of ions and free electrons and is able to reflect radio waves. This was discovered in 1925 and it exists at ~ 80 kms height from earth. Ionization is due to solar flares/sun spot activity. Its band width is at +ve voltage of 500,000 volts! The earth is a negative pole to the field of ionosphere. The system becomes a "ball condenser". The gap in between acts as a waveguide with wavelength = earths circumference.

Schumann measured resonance at 7.83 Hz in 1954. Harmonics are at 6.5 Hz apart at 14.3, 20.8, 27.3 algorhythmically. These resonant waves are continuously excited by ~100 lightning discharges every second of day! It can, therefore, be said that 7.83 Hz is earths "heart beat" frequency!

Physicians immediately noted the similarity between the waves observed in mammalian brain EEG patterns and the Schumann resonances. The alpha waves during human brain activity lie in the same frequency range as the first two modes of the Schumann resonance. It is attributed to human adaptation to the electro-magnetic environment in the course of evolution over millions of years. Much research is underway in this inter-disciplinary area between physics, biology and medicine. It is established for sure that electro-magnetic waves do affect the brain.

However, it is established that there is a mysterious role of 7.8 Hz frequency. Fourier analysis (frequency spectrum) of EEG patterns of 30 different healers shows a sharp peak close to 7.8 Hz. This may explain placebo effect, effect of belief on biological systems and, may be *shamamic* healing.

IMPLICATIONS FOR DISTANT HEALING

Molecular Effect Resonance Technology (MRET)

This is a real life situation. There was a disastrous nuclear radiation leak at Chernobyl, A Russian scientist, *Igor Smirnov* and his team was called in by the Soviet government to research the healing effects of certain mountain springs on victims of the radioactive fallout. For centuries local people used these healing springs. What was it about the water that could actually help victims of radiation exposure? Through Nuclear Magnetic Resonance Tests and IR Spectroscopy Smirnov discovered unique healing secrets of the spring water. There was unusual configuration and high-energy activity of water molecules. Smirnov then developed a technology that could replicate this amazing natural process and patented it. He called it MRET. He postulated Molecular Resonance Effect Technology, creates a subtle low frequency field that closely resembles the natural geomagnetic field found near healing water springs. Water is exposed to magnetic field and oscillating optical light of 600 nm wavelength and 7.8 Hz frequency. It retains effect for several months; This was the phenomenon of memory of water. A similar finding was reported in the journal *Nature* - 1987. This was later withdrawn.

Paranormal Phenomena

Researchers belonging to different disciplines such as experimental physics, electrical engineering and biology have joined parapsychologists in investigating paranormal phenomena such as telepathy, extra sensory perception (ESP), clairvoyance, remote viewing, psycho-kinesis (PK), mind-matter interaction etc. Considerable evidence has also been accumulated of telepathy and ESP in animals by Rupert Sheldrake.

Subtle Energies

The unknown information transfer mechanisms in all these phenomena, involving interaction between mind and mind, or between mind and distant places or between mind and matter, has been characterized in scientific circles by the all embracing term "Subtle Energies". Thus the mechanism of various energy healing techniques such as Pranic healing, Reiki, distant healing etc. is attributed to the role of Subtle Energies.

The evolving field of Consciousness research has been described by some investigators as being "The Last Frontier" of Science while others are referring to the advances being made in understanding Consciousness related phenomena as "The Third Scientific Revolution".

There are two distinct approaches that scientists have adopted to understand Consciousness related phenomena: These can be categorized as (i) Brain-centric (or localized approach).

This assumes that consciousness is limited to the brain. Its proponents assert that there is nothing to consciousness beyond the "firing of the neurons". (ii) The second viewpoint contends that consciousness extends well beyond the brain emphasizing its "non-local" feature (as evident in paranormal and subtle energy phenomena).

SCIENTIFIC INVESTIGATIONS OF NON-LOCAL MANIFESTATIONS OF CONSCIOUSNESS

Remote Viewing (RV)

Some gifted people have the extraordinary psychic ability to see things at a far off distance—clairvoyance. Obviously this is extra-sensory perception (ESP). This is documented by Patanjali as the first of his Ashta Siddhis—eight exceptional faculties. *Anima* translates as the "ability to acquire knowledge of the small, the hidden and the distant. In scientific literature this property is categorized as Remote Viewing. It is verified by researchers at Princeton University's "PEAR" programme. The results confirmed the ability of psychics to go into the future several hours ahead of time. These findings confirm that the non-local characteristics of consciousness not only extends in space but also in time.

Concept of Akashic Records

Another important observation in RV experiments was that once in a while the remote viewer while describing the scene being witnessed by the agent, would accidentally describe features of the target site which were not present at the time of the viewing, but had existed decades or centuries ago. This corroborates the concept of "Akashic Records", namely that every event or incident that happens in the world at every place and at every moment gets etched in subtle space—*Akash.* with clairvoyant vision can describe past events in great detail. Edgar Casey and C.W. Leadbeater have written many articles. These claims now appear more believable following the scientific corroborations emanating from RV research.

Remote viewing of the objects that were destroyed long ago; and, are still visualized by the remote viewer as if they are there generates an argument in favour of consciousness being the Fifth Dimension in physics. That means that consciousness is not confined to a specific space-time location. Fourth dimension in physics enunciates space-time continuity that is straight in our ordinary perception of the world. It gets curvilinear in astronomical observations. However, consciousness seems to be not confined to a particular location and, can move forward and backwards as well. Then only a remote viewer will be able to "see" now non-existent objects that have been destroyed long back.

Some degree of scientific validity to the technique of distant healing is provided by RV research stemming from non-locality of consciousness. In actual case studies carried out under controlled conditions, this does not appear to be statistically persuasive.

MIND-MATTER INTERACTION PHENOMENA

Extra Sensory Perception (ESP) and Spoon Bending

Clairvoyance, clairaudience, psychokinesis—influencing matter without touching it, such as spoon bending are known to occur. The scientific community has always been skeptical. That some people have faculties to mentally influence matter and *Raj Yoga* practice not only generates insight but ESP and even prognostication, are facts that can some day be explained only by quantum physics.

Study of Distant Influence of Qi-gong Masters

A related study is the scientific investigation of the psycho kinetic powers of "Qi-gong Masters in Japan (with government funding) and in China. The master is asked to send a pulse of psychic energy directed at the subject simultaneously mark this time on the computer. Subsequent analysis of the data obtained from the subject's body sensors indicate that the diagnostic sensors indicate that several body parameters get perturbed.

Random Number Generator Experiments

The choice of 0 or 1 state of a digital electronic circuit driven by a naturally random process involves a device that operates on computation. Experiments at the Princeton University's PEAR lab, confirmed that student volunteers were able to mentally influence a piece of matter, namely the RNG. It appeared to be sensitive to the feeling of love between two human participants. It was this interesting finding that led to the next stage of the programme, namely the study of "field effects" or "group consciousness effects."

Field Effects Studies

What could be the mechanism by which a human mind is able to influence the properties of a Random Number Generator from a distance? For this we invoke the concept of a "field". It is proposed that there is a "consciousness field—a quantum field" associated with and surrounding every mind.

Global Consciousness Project

Roger Nelson previously of the Princeton PEAR group are testing a hypothesis through Global Consciousness Project (GCP). They have created a global network of computers monitoring the whole world's group consciousness field on a round the clock basis.

The most impressive result of the GCP network (maximum deviation from purely random behaviour) observed occurred on 11th September 2001 (the infamous 9/11 incident). The quantum of deviation of the data from normal behaviour peaked sharply at around 8.45 am, precisely when the first plane crashed into the first skyscraper. However, a most puzzling feature of the result was that the deviation started to increase even before the plane actually crashed into the building. This indicates that the GCP network of computers appeared to have displayed an aspect of pre-cognition of the events!

IIED Experiments

William Tiller, formerly at Stanford University has carried out a series of psycho-energetic experiments which demonstrated that a group of meditators is able to consciously implant a specific intention into a special electronic device. A typical intention they used is for the electrical device to acquire the ability to "increase" (or alternatively "decrease") the *p*H of a bottle of ultra pure water placed near it. It is found that the *p*H of the water increases (or decrease as the case may be) by one full *p*H unit, over a one week period, exactly as envisaged by the implanted intention.

Tiller thus extends Einstein's postulate of the equivalence of mass and energy to a third component of reality. Considering that consciousness is also a form of energy, he postulates the reciprocity as follows:

MATTER→ ENERGY→ CONSCIOUSNESS and *vice versa.*

ESP Study of Nuclear Structure

One important piece of work is the remarkable clairvoyant investigations into the detailed structure of atoms and nuclei (Table 5.2). This was carried out by the theosophists Annie

Besant and C.W. Leadbeater over a century ago. This proves that yogic method of knowing reality directly is a faculty that does happen. Using psycho-kinetic thought processes, Annie Besant disintegrated the atom in her field of view until she arrived at what she called a single ultimate particle atom-UPA. Using further magnification Leadbeater described the structure of each UPA. This correlates to the present day knowledge of subatomic particles.

Table 5.2: Observations by C.W. Leadbeater and Annie Besant

1895	positive and negative hydrogen triplets observed in MPAs	1864	Quark model proposes nuclei are made up of 2 positive u quarks and 1 negative d quark and also in reverse mode
1908	meta-neon (number weight = 22.33);	1912	Neon-22 discovered
1908	axes of UPAs observed to be aligned by electric field; UPAs depicted as joined by lines of force of a magnetic nature;	1933	magnetic monopoles with possible electric dipole moments discussed by Dirac
1908	some UPAs shown as end points of single lines of force	1970	String model of hadrons; quarks regarded as ends of strings or flux tubes
1908	Y shaped configurations of lines of force ending on UPA published	1975	Baryons modeled as Y-shaped strings with quarks at their ends
1909	"illinium" (number weight = 146.66);	1945	promethium-147 discovered
1909	"masurium" (number weight = 100.11)	1937	technitium-99 discovered
1924	processional motions of 'hydrogen triangles' (protons)	1924	spin of nuclei suggested
1932	element 85 (number weight = 221.00); element 87 (number weight 222.55)	1940	astatine 219 discovered 1939 francium 223 discovered.

Source: Occult Chemistry, CW Leadbeater and Annie Beasant, Theosophical Publishing House, 1905.

The original observations as recorded by Besant and Leadbeater, and the remarkable interpretation of the same in terms of the most up-to-date concepts of contemporary particle physics strike wonder for all. We cannot but be overawed by the minuteness and depth to which Besant and Leadbeater appear to have been able to delve into the intricacies of the structure of the matter.

Micro-Sensing in Jain Tradition (Table 5.3)

The above phenomena are only a century old. The prophet of Jain religion, Mahavir was born about 2500 years ago and Jain and Buddhist traditions are more or less contemporaries. Both the traditions generated an occult discipline. There is immaculate description of atoms and sub-atomic particles in the books of Jain tradition too. The original books are by Umasvati and Hemchandracharya. The texts are a thousand years old. The recently published versions give original *Pali* version and its translation. In the translations of this kind, there are possibilities of differences in semantic interpretation. Even then, the observations are strikingly similar to leave us spell bound.

Stephen Phillips compared the occult observations with the modern understanding of nuclear structure such as the quark theory of matter. Phillips has showed that Besant and Leadbeater's observations are in excellent quantitative agreement with contemporary quarks and superstring model of matter. One off-shoot of these studies has been the recognition, especially in "New Age" circles, of the potential power of meditation and synchronized (or coherent) group thought processes. The evidence emanating from these studies concede that modern science has missed out on some important facets of reality. For the believers, the facts narrated may hardly matter; they were convinced through their own experience of trance in *turya.* For the skeptics, they will have to wait till quantum physics and biological sciences provide

Table 5.3: Micro-PSI Visualization in Jain Tradition

1. That which is matter (*pud)* and yet it disappears (*galan).* is the smallest of the small particle of matter (*pudgal).*	In 1924, de Broglie (1894-1987) described the theory of wave particle duality for which he was awarded Nobel prize in 1929. An electron when detached from the atom, it is called free electron and free electron theory treats electrons as freely moving.
2. That consciousness which is non-dual is also *pudgal.*	Not established in physics so far. Consonant with our hypothesis that consciousness is a field and an additional dimension
3. By the union of *pudgal* with each other, the gross matter arises.	Protons and electrons were discovered by the beginning of 20th century and in 1932, neutrons were discovered as the fundamental constituents of matter.
4. Though *pudgal* is beyond the definition of origin, middle or end, since it has a charge (*ekpradeshi)*, it can be said to have a direction.	According to quantum theory as postulated by Planck (1858-1947), elementary particles have a spin in a particular direction. This won him Nobel Prize in 1918.
5. One that cannot be pierced or divided by the sharpest instrument and one that cannot be destroyed	Strong nuclear force, responsible for holding together of positively charged protons and neutral neutrons was postulated in 1930 and established in 1940.
6. By the combination of eight subtle (*sannasana)* subparticles, one *pudgal* is produced.	Yukava (1907-81), a Japanese physicist predicted in 1930 that there is a fundamental force holding the nucleus of an atom together. He called it a "middle weight" before it was termed as meson. The nuclear force between protons and neutrons is termed strong interaction. Gel Mann (1929-) in 1964 proposed the eightfold way to define the structure of particles.
7. *Pudgal* may exist as a particle or a field	This is the basic principle of quantum theory. See Schrodinger's cat experiment and Heisenberg's uncertainty principle discussed above.
8. By the dissolution of a combination (*skandha),* that indivisible element which is obtained, is the active *pudgal;*	Hadrons are a class of subatomic particles. They are made of quarks.

(*Contd.*)

9. From the coming together of various *pudgals,* a combination *(skandha)* is brought about	It is various combinations of quarks that constitute matter. In 1978, a standard model for the constitution of all matter was established as that of leptons, quarks and mediators.
10. *Pudgals* with flavour and colour are described and they change themselves from one state to other.	Quarks combine with each other through affinity that is determined by 'colour charge'. The theory governing these colour charge combinations is called quantum chromodynamics. Various 'flavors' are also ascribed to quarks. These advances have occurred between 1961-64-74-78-1998.
11. A *pudgal* is not inactive; it exists in a dynamic state.	Subatomic particles are ascribed a particular spin.
12. In one space only a single *pudgal* can exist. But, if it is paired, the pair may exist in a single location in space.	Pauli's (1900-1958) exclusion principle formulated in 1924-25, states that no two identical particles in a system can exist in the same space. He won the Nobel prize in 1945. Dirac (1902-1984) derived the equation that postulated existence of a positron – antielectron in 1927. They have the same mass but opposite charge. He won the Nobel prize in 1933: Youngest to win the prize so far, he has to his credit largest number of his students winning the prize.
13. *Pudgal* has property to combine; that shows that it is active	See 8,9, 10 above
14. The infinitely vast space and the infinitesimal small *pudgal* are two expressions of same reality.	Space is supposed to be filled with infinite energy field; a small undulation in this field materializes the matter (*vide supra*)

further leads or, may be through some suffering that brings about symptom path to enlightenment.

The implicate order in the matter and the subtleties of consciousness will now be studied further in 21st century with quantum physics. Experiments at the Large Hedron Collider in 2012 promised a generation of higher grade of computation with computers. By 2016 a virtual re-creation of Big Bang is computerized. Therefore, it is irrelevant now to turn to occult practices to unravel the mysteries of Universe. Now that more and many Steve Jobs roam through the Himalayas and gaze at the sky, the descent of gratuitous graces on them will bring about more magnanimous discoveries. The software of such creation is available with *Raj Yoga*. We shall study them in later chapters.

The answer shall be through a future Einstein who shall discover "conscion" that will generate Unified Single Theory of four fundamental theories in physics and, by the future *vajrasattva* Buddha and Patanjali who will teach the methods of experiencing and enhancing quantum electrodynamic fields. That will validate the hypothesis that consciousness is primordial and universal. The individual is a fragment from the whole. When the fragment-individual consciousness-unites with universal, Fifth Dimension to the Reality will come into play. That will explain all the paranormal phenomena either occurring spontaneously or as revelations of hidden faculties through *Raj Yoga* practice.

Chapter 6

Gratuitous Graces: Creativity and Beyond

Creativity and some other phenomena occur spontaneously through the meditation. The scientific basis of such insights has been discussed in the previous chapter. We shall understand them further.

We have understood mindfulness. With this strategy, the meditator minds his mind to remain in the present. Mind does not—not allowed to—wander. Past events are absolute: they cannot be undone. Rumination over them is a waste of mental energy. Thinking of what to do next time or day is likely not to materialize. We do not have control on the future. Minding the mind at the present moment is just a simple and easily acceptable method for meditation. One may begin there and, is surely to progress to wider vistas. Its limitation is that there is much more to experience beyond mind. However, the benefits accrue regardless.

Insight, intuition, inspiration, creativity and refined aesthetics are immediate rewards to a meditator. A hunch or intuition arises in the mind without a rational didactic process. There is no logical validation immediately. There are neither logical steps to generate intuition. Yet intuition differs from any irrational belief by the fact that it comes out as a future event or a fact: while superstitions are soon belied. When Archimedes cried out " Aha", he was in the altered state of consciousness. That is how the intuitive answers arrive—like the flash of lightening.

The generation of insight is not accomplished by any amount of toil. The process of didactic, dialectic, and discursive logic can lead to critical thinking. That will provide logical answers. This is restricted to the left hemisphere functioning of the brain. Poetical truth, justice and aesthetics are experienced by the mankind since ages. This prevailed even before the age of reason dawned in the West. Meditation makes the flowering of creativity. This *happens* in the generic ground of Fourth State—*turya*—that is full of wonder, joy, beauty, expectation and ecstasy. Truth is beauty and beauty is joy.

We shall see only one such example. There is a time-honoured model, Einstein—as to how his intuition *arrived.*

EINSTEIN A MODEL

Einstein describes the experience of intense creativity through insight and intuition in response to a query from Hadamard. Einstein admitted to getting into a different state of mind in his creative moments. He has described it as thinking with the symbols. This is reproduced verbatim as:

> My Dear Colleague,
> In the following, I am trying to answer in brief your questions as well as I am able. I am not satisfied myself with those answers and I am willing to answer more questions if you believe this could be of any advantage for the very interesting and difficult work you have undertaken.

(A) The words or the language, as they are written or spoken, do not seem to play any role in my mechanism of thought. The psychical entities, which seem to serve as elements in thought are certain signs and more or less clear images that can be "voluntarily" reproduced and combined.

There is, of course, a certain connection between those elements and relevant logical concepts. It is also clear that the desire to arrive finally at logically connected concepts is the emotional basis of this rather vague play with the above-mentioned elements. But taken from a psychological viewpoint, this combinatory play seems to be the essential feature in productive thought—before there is any connection with logical construction in words or other kind of signs that can be communicated to others.

(B) The above-mentioned elements are, in my case, of visual and some muscular type. Conventional words or other signs have to be sought for laboriously only in a secondary stage, when the mentioned associative play is sufficiently established and can be reproduced at will.

(C) According to what has been said, the play with the mentioned elements is aimed to be analogous to certain logical connections one is searching for.

(D) Visual and motor. In a stage when words intervene at all, they are, in my case, purely auditive, but they interfere only in a secondary stage as already mentioned.

From the above letter, it is obvious that the experience described is akin to a meditative state. Thus, *turya is* a ground state for creativity. That is seen with the experience of Einstein. Of course, it does not matter that he may have not even known such a word. Even before him, William James in 1892 described the varieties of religious experiences. His studies even today are widely read. James was probably the first scientist to try to convenience his fraternity that mystic experiences are actual happenings. James recognized an uniformity in the saintly experiences, be it an experience by saint Paul, Saint Augustin or other saints of his time. James concluded that the visualizations of, and visitation by guardian angels may have come from inside. The mind of the saint or may *have been from God.* James concluded that such experiences transform life. There is a similarity of this experiences with *turya* in classical Indian tradition, that is an experience that states that I am one with the Whole—*aham brahmasmi.* Human beings on different grounds of religiosity and cultural tradition may name the altered state of consciousness differently. *De facto* they were indeed spiritual experiences of saints.

LUMINOSITY AND CHARISMA THROUGH INTUITIVE INSIGHT

The meditative experience creates luminosity so that there is charisma around the person. Health is preserved. We have already seen stress reduction and its molecular biology. Moreover, any dis-ease that may arise from the faulty functioning of discriminating wisdom of intellect (Charak, the first physician of Ayurveda, propounded: *all diseases arise from faulty functioning of pragyna*—intuitive functioning of intellect) may also be rectified. Distress comes to be eustress. This is through the intuitive insight in meditative state. We study a model developed by Kathryn Rossi for creativity enhancement as well as for application in therapeutic hypnosis.

We have a model, developed by Kathryn Rossi, for enhancing creativity as well as its application for therapeutic hypnosis.

FOUR STAGE CREATIVE CYCLE: KATHRYN ROSSI

Ernest and Kathryn Rossi have developed a Four Stage Creative Cycle utilizing natures natural psychobiological 90-120-minute Basic Rest and Activity Cycle (BRAC). Stage One is curiosity and engagement with a question, a problem or an interest. Stage Two is when the person works through puzzling questions and may involve considerable effort. Stage Three is the "*Aha*!" realization of possible creative solutions that may include enlightenment. Stage Four is when we put it all together for practical applications in daily life.

Kathryn Rossi has developed a model of practice consistent with Patanjali's eight limbed *yoga* utilizing 90-120 minute ultradian cycles. Originally, Ernest Rossi was inspired by Milton Erickson practiced unusually long psychotherapy sessions of 90-120 minutes. When asked why he did so Erickson said, "That is the time it takes to get something done!" Whereas a circadian cycle is of 24 hours, the 90-120-minute ultradian cycle is how we get things done. Going with our natural biological rhythms facilitates *turya*, generation of the Fourth State of Consciousness. Ultradian shifts of consciousness can often be observed with the alternating flow of the breath through the left (*ida*) and right (*pingala*) nostrils.

There is spacious speculation about the psychic organs of the *chakras, kundalini yoga* etc. The practice merges into *tantrika* domain and we shall have an overview later. At the present there is good reason to seek and measure all states of human consciousness development with advanced and sensitive measurements. The scientific progress though slow, is ongoing. We welcome any *idea whose time has come*! We are confident, continued studies will illuminate the best ways to grow and evolve human consciousness at large. Kathryn and Ernest Rossi have focused to a large number of people with therapeutic applications of hypnosis.

HYPNOSIS AND THERAPEUTIC APPLICATIONS

A meditator spontaneously develops a natural faculty to induce trance in others. This is hypnosis. This may be utilized for treatment. During hypnosis control is within the individual. The hypnotherapist is simply there to help facilitate their natural trance. Much speculation has led to a misunderstanding that the therapist controls the client. The simple truth is nobody can be hypnotized against his/her will. Of course, there are stories of gullible subjects having been taken advantage by pseudo-saints. In the present age, therapeutic hypnotherapy is developed as a modern scientific specialty. Many hypnotherapists learn to treat a broad spectrum of physical and emotional conditions through scientific discipline. All the better if the hypnotherapist has an understanding and practice of *Raj Yoga*. (*See* Table 5.1, Chapter 5)

Rapport building has much relevance in therapy and has a vital significance. In therapeutic relationships, there are communions in consciousness between the participants. The co-creative process between the therapist and client is often restorative.

Though hypnosis was known in India since antiquity, it was Milton Erickson who laid foundations for modern therapeutic hypnosis. Kathryn Rossi follows nature to lead to facilitate new consciousness in therapeutic sessions using the Four Stage Creative Cycle. The session often concludes with a heightened sense of creativity. The client may find a cure from a disease or, perhaps a new and better way to express creative efforts to be their best self; rather than through a neurotic compensation that manifest as a disease. Thus, the disease may just be a symptom of dysfunctionality and, this symptom may open up a path to enlightenment. One definition of *Yoga* is the attainment of highest functionality.

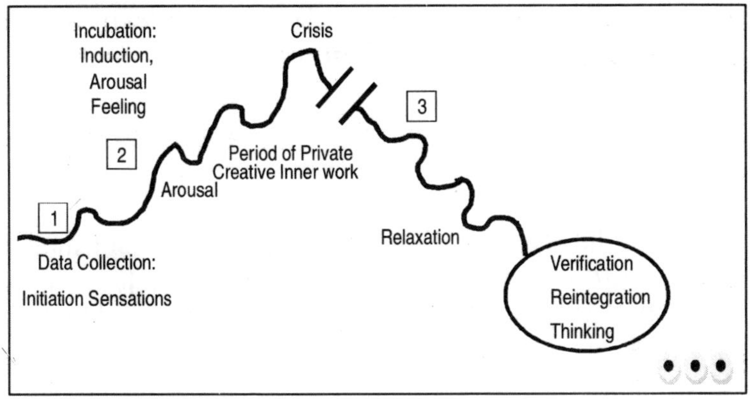

Fig. 6.1: Classical 90-120-minute therapeutic hypnosis session. (Rossi, 2002, The Psychobiology of Gene Expression: Neuroscience and Neurogenesis in Hypnosis and the Healing Arts. Used with Permission).

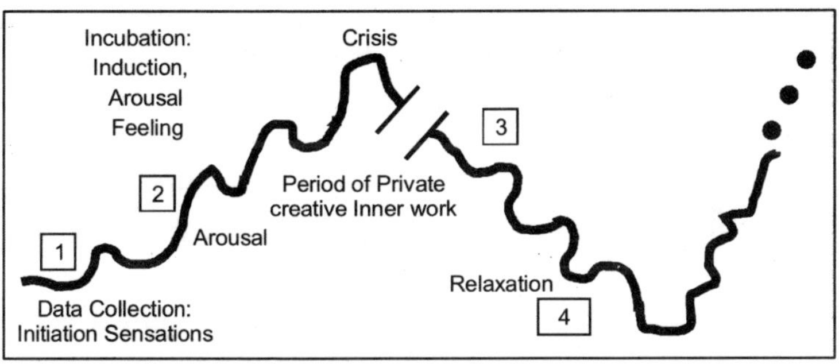

Fig. 6.2: Authors' Modification based on long term *Raj Yoga* practice

NUMINOUS IMAGES AND GUIDING ANGELS

The creative process gets further refined through utilization of imagery with symbols. With symbols lead to specific insight generation as per their archetypal sensibilities with the subject. This leads to resolve ones conflicts. We have been using this technique for hypnotherapy and employ such images as per the subject's cultural conditioning. The process does require reinforcement and the insight to occur as instantaneous flash, but eventually it does arise either a flash or a gentle trickle of a ray of light. Jung's subjects experienced a kind of luminosity during transcendent imagination. The numinous images came up in these subjects spontaneously and their spiritual quality made Jung to think that this was away to connect to divinity or God.

This is illustrated by the following example, What happens to the mind/in the brain of the person who creatively attempts to visualize the image of Goddess Sarasvati? Visualization of the creative symbol of Sarasvati in all its magnificent splendour and associated paraphernalia expounds a meaning of learning and erudition, Serenity, peaceful joy and creative wisdom in the minds of all belonging to the Indian ethos. In the process, it may facilitate learning and scholarship. Such interpretation contributes to the semantic thesis of Searle. However, as the process is transcribed in the brain cells, it will have to undergo several stages of molecular biological events in progression. This will be particularly so when the holographic integration of inputs of all the senses happens. The memory in the brain is in the form of engram over a wide area of the brain. So, as the meaning to the creative visualization of a symbol becomes obvious, interaction between nth number of engrams is most likely to have occurred by the time that the creative process has yielded a result.

We have emphasized on the cultural conditioning of the subjects. However present day connectivity has expanded to the extent that there is a development of a holographic culture for the humanity through the internet. This is illustrated by the fact that Kathryn Rossi utilizes the symbol of Hanuman to generate affirmation and strength during her sessions.

Thus, intuition is not just a delayed recall. Nor it is plumbing or ploughing of the unconscious. It seems to arise from a background state of silence arising by stopping the clutter in the mind. At every moment, ordinarily, several thoughts roam in the mind from what happened to what is likely to happen. Every single thought process takes sometime and energy. Unfinished agenda keeps on peeping out of sub-conscious mind. When a computer is simultaneously working with several programmes, it does slow down. This is applicable to the brain. Though unconscious mind is ordinarily not at the surface, it lies repressed. It is comparable to the pressure in a pressure cooker. Taking the analogy to the computer, dynamic demi-urgic forces of the unconscious mind are like silent viruses in the software of the brain.

Even at the stage of mindfulness meditation, where the focus of the mind is on the present moment, above factors are eliminated. While focusing on the present moment, each moment of reflection causes a generation of a single quantum dynamic field—QED. Progressing in an algorithm, several such synchronous fields superimpose to arrive at the flash. Intuition thus may be said to be the product of the super-impositions—summation of several QEDs.

We have arrived at a step where we can now conceive intuition being a creative endeavour. What is of further relevance is that such a processing is facilitated by altered state of consciousness/meditation. While one cannot cultivate intuition so as to reveal itself at will, it can at least be approached through meditation. This expansion of consciousness can extend to esoteric and, even occult fields of consciousness. Classically, Patanjali refers to development of eight faculties. They extend into subtle realms of consciousness and, are beyond the scope of mind. Sanskrit words, *Anima, Mahima, Laghima, Garima, Prapti, Prakamya, Ishita* and *Vashita* have been translated differently by various *Pandits.*

Rather than entering into a debate about semantics, we may consider *Anima* and *Laghima* as the faculties to see small and minutest of matter. This was developed and practiced by Annie Besant and C.W. Leadbeater and, published as well. Stephan Phillips examined and proved the validity of their findings. This is of relevance so as to inspire awe and respect. *Mahima* and *Garima* are best interpreted as the glory, charisma and aura about the personality of the meditator. It will be appropriate to discuss *Prapti, Prakamya,* and *Ishita* respectively meaning faculty to achieve, to materialize what is wished and to create as willed, to discuss later. It is pertinent to discuss *Vashita*—to control mind of others here as it overlaps creativity.

PARANORMAL HEALING

Healing or therapy with hypnosis is now well established scientific discipline. *Raj Yogis* have been helping people to heal—cure in a mystic way from time immemorial till today. Prayers have helped patients since ages. Dora Kunz developed a technique that she called therapeutic touch. This will have a probable scientific basis in the form of arousal of different set of genes J. Krishnamurthy was told by Annie Besant that his hands have power to heal. He is known to have done so to several people. Rohit Mehta had paralysis while in prison. Krishnamurthy visited him three times in the hospital and touched his spine. Rohit Mehta not only recovered fully but himself developed a strategy to heal patients. Another well known example is that of Vimla Thakar. After being cured from her chronic ear problem, she lived as a *Raj Yogi* for the rest of her life.

Rohit Mehta taught us how to utilize transfer of energy to a patient as follows:

16 March, 1986

My Dear Rajni,

Thank you very much for writing to us seeking clarifications about certain matters that we had discussed. I wish we had more sittings together. The matters that you have raised need to be discussed rather than dealt with in a letter. But there are two things that need to be born in mind: i. the whole image therapy is in an experimental stage. ii. No clear-cut method therefore can be indicated. The experiment has to go on for sometime all over the world before any thing positive can emerge. Here the experiments must be both by medical people as also by lay people.

It has to be remembered that we are dealing with human beings and not with machines. No static approach will ever do and all the methods have to be very tentative. Each human being is unique and, therefore, his problems and situations are also unique. They cannot be put in the framework of the average. Each human case has to be approached a new each time.

Bearing this in mind, we have to explore a threefold approach or method.

There has to be a self-experiment. Each medical person must experiment this approach personally first. For this he may take up some small problem in his or her own life and see whether image-treatment helps. Or he may experiment on some healthy person with reference to some comparatively small problem. If the approach of the image therapy helps, then one may vary the experiment and see whether image therapy enables the physician himself to make his self free from a particular psychological difficulty.

The physician who has thus far tested the validity of this approach can experiment on some patient not involved in any serious ailments. But, for this experiment there must be a perfect rapport between the doctor and the patient. It must be rapport of person to person, not between the patient and a professional. In this state the doctor can try the image therapy and move along in a clear and systematic manner.

The experiment on the patient must be on the following lines.

- The patient must be induced to relax with the help of soft music or chanting of mantras or may be by showing the pictures or slides of natural beauty.
- The patient must be induced to relate his life story. He must speak about incidences and experiences in his own life but not about the ailment. The life story should be narrated clearly and as far as possible chronologically.
- Taking cue from the patient's narration, the doctor can pick up some positive element about the patient's capability. The doctor can put the question along the positive lines creating within the patient a sense of confidence, making him aware of what this can do.
- The doctor can then describe to the patient varying circumstances of life, describing in as detail a manner as possible and watch patient's reactions and responses. In fact the patient must be exposed to the description of circumstances and events involving people with whom the patient is related.

The patient may now be asked to lie down with closed eyes, or just be quietly relaxed, or may even dose off. It is now that the doctor can utilize the image therapy experiment as follows:

- The doctor must be in a state of complete relaxation—he must evolve his own method to relax.
- The doctor must create within himself a release of more energy. He must clearly and intensely visualize some

happy moments—something, which evokes pleasure.

- He then concentrates on patient's condition free from the particular illness. Visualize strongly and intensely that the patient is free from his illness. Actually see the patient moving about in a perfectly happy and healthy state.
- The doctor must now sit completely quiet and silent for sometime releasing as it were the image of health that he had formed of the patient.

After regular experimentation for a few days, the patient may be induced to do self-healing. Here the patient can be slowly trained to the fourfold process of image therapy viz.

- conservation of energy-relaxation,
- creation of new energy visualizing something immensely pleasurable,
- concentrating this fresh energy on some spots of illness visualizing their complete cure, and
- communication of the visualized images in complete silence.

In brief, image therapy must follow three fundamental steps: (i) self-experimentation, (ii) doctor's projection of healthy image on the patient, and (iii) inducing the patient himself to do the healing.

Theosophists perform a ritual to help patients from a distance. At this stage it is appropriate to mention that fourth state of consciousness is the gateway to the fifth dimension where the conventional space-time dimension takes a quantum jump into five dimensional, space-time-consciousness continuum. The importance of archetypal symbols, that rests on the concept of collective consciousness, is to see consciousness as the energy in a wave/field form; a wave/field that has no particulate matter incorporated, or it may have subatomic particles of the size of photon (0 mass). Such a wave will travel at the speed of light. It is not known, and with high profile science available to us today, it is not necessary to know how the development of special faculties happen. The relevance is that they did happen. And it is useful to know how some evolved people did accomplish this rare, esoteric kind of gratuitous grace to descend on them.

Chapter 7

Pratyahara: Negation of Random Thoughts

Unwelcome Guests; closure of multiple programmes and "Open Sesame"!

The concept of *pratyahara* would need greater elucidation and wider exploration for the novice. It includes how to shun unwelcome guests: closure of multiple programmes. Simultaneously, there is transition to *turya.* When it initially happens to the novice, it is almost alike the first step of Alice in wonderland. A panorama of whole, new, brave world unfolds. There is showering of the happy molecules so that *ananda*—ecstasy pervades each and every cell of the body.

We need to further understand the mind, its manipulations and how to calm it down to progress to meditative state.

We have reviewed the data regarding meditation in compartments so far. It may appear diverse and mystic. Science and spiritually may seem to be just weakly connected. For scientific validation, singing by a single cuckoo does not mean heralding of the spring. For spiritual experience, a moment may express what the heavens toiled to express for ages! But the integration of both the aspects is possible. While the understanding neuro-science may buttress belief—and belief initiates faith—an experience of *turya* is enough to convince every- one that there are other states of consciousness than those we ordinary are aware.

What is discussed so far provides a ground state that there are empirical proofs available about a fourth state of awareness where, paranormal phenomena do occur.

PANORAMA BEYOND MIND: SUBTLE FORMS OF SELF

Most people have a habitual, culturally conditioned style of living. Indian tradition describes physical body as having five different forms. What is seen is physical form sustained through food etc. But there are four other subtle forms.

We restrict our deliberations to the mental level. This is a common level of existence for most of us. Our functionality is through the refinement of intellect and, rationalizations arrived from there. This would be fine if it stops with the development of critical thinking. But life is full of vicissitudes. And, we saw earlier in Chapter 3 as to how mind derives various neurotic attitudes to cope with them. That is Freudian psychoanalysis.

Indian concepts are further relevant. Apart from our physical body, there is a subtle form—energy form. They both keep on undergoing change from time to time through the influence of the environment and the events in the surrounding. Consequently, there is a dynamic change in the energy form and mental concepts. The changes invariably influence the discriminating wisdom. The impairment of discrimination surely endangers the natural joyful state that should be one's fundamental attribute. For those who believe in the *carmic* connections, this could be what has been accumulated and stored for long in unconscious mind—that equates with *chitta*. For the believer in a designed argument for the Universe such an event was bound to happen. Thus, it may be attributed to destiny.

MIND: SIXTH SENSE ORGAN

It is obvious that all of us keep doing some activity for the life time. The functionality is dependent on the sense organs. However, Indian Classical tradition enunciates a Sixth sense organ. That is *manas*.

The nature has organized the functions of the sense organs for self preservation. Yet, it is common knowledge that pleasure is associated with the functions of all five senses. And, it is generally not known, but widely practiced that pleasure seeking can happen with the singular activity of mind as well.

Pratyahar is a conscious activity to bridle the senses. The senses do and must function for the preservation of self. However, they cannot and, must not indulge into an endless pleasure seeking. Such endeavour will tune the senses to a refined aesthetic appreciation without indulgence. Obviously, this is different from making senses dull and deaf. That would physically harm.

The intention is to so refine the senses that there is tremendous joy from a little of perfect performance.

In short, *Pratyahar* is described as withdrawal of all senses including mind. And, withdrawal of mind would mean withdrawal from projections and compensations that it derives from neurotic manipulations. Blavetsky advised constant wiping the mirror of the mind to keep it clean. That alone will safeguard discriminative, wise judgments from time to time.

INTERPRETATION OF EGO: WEST AND EAST

This brings us to a distinctively different understanding of self-ego from Western psychology. The latter defines ego as a psychic concept that constantly strives to balance between the irrational and, may be anti-social demands of id and, restrictive, conservative commands of super ego that may be culturally conditioned. Obviously, if we subscribe to this then, one is under a constant threat. On the other hand, Indian Psychology considers that, in reality, there is no such person that is, " I—the doer". An individual is just an instrument. All actions and effects arising out of the instrument are ordained. Or, they happen as a consequence to numerous forces acting upon the individual. It should be understood that this is not a denial of responsibility; it only relieves the burden of the past. One may find this in synchrony with *ishwara pranidhana* that we discussed earlier.

INSTANT REPLAY IN MIND

Indian tradition, as said before and repeated for emphasis here, defines mind as the sixth sense organ. Mind is continuously active. Through its associative property with other senses as well as its commutation and computation with pre-conceived concepts, it is in constant replay mode. It is common knowledge for the computer literate that running several programmes simultaneously at one time slows down the speed of the computer. We discussed mindfulness that emphasizes living in the present moment. That should also mean exclusion of not only the past memories and future expectations, but focusing only on the action at the hand at a given time. Shunning and shutting all other thoughts than those that are pertinent at a given moment—time—action, is *pratyahara*.

However, this takes some practice.

UNWELCOME GUESTS

While practicing meditation constant attempts to shut out different thoughts will result in their coming from several other directions. The strategy is to treat all the thoughts—except what is to be meditated upon—as unwelcome guest. They are guest;

howsoever unwelcome. They cannot be pushed away. But, unwelcome guest need not be entertained by any kind of ceremonious welcome. They need to be left alone. This way, unwelcome guest depart by themselves.

Mind become quite and, slowly and passively it allows *turya* to descend.

DESCENT OF *TURYA*

The awareness of the material universe, through and beyond the fourth state, *turya*, appears to be entirely different than what we usually perceive. Now as we begin to integrate the compartmentalized understanding, the duality between the observer and observed will slowly dissolve at the culmination of *Samadhi.* One can be impatient and ask: when and how it will happen etc.

Meditation can be a cyclic process. We have seen that Patanjali enunciates eight steps. But they are not to be understood as stages in progression. First step is the last step! A few people like Socrates and Ramakrishna Paramhans went into meditation spontaneously. J. Krishnamurthy maintained, "It happens", and, at times he remained in the altered state for days together. For most people let there be a regular practice for about 20 minutes twice a day. Let there be a quiet and passive acceptance of such happenings. For a functional, socially productive, creative person in 21st century, mysticism is accepted and, need not be further dissected. A rose is a rose is a rose. Integration of several different psychodynamic and scientific processes is arrived at by just an experience. It grows with practice. Sugar will taste the same sweet; without analyzing why dextrose tastes so.

PANORAMA BEYOND MIND

Sri Aurobindo described a higher mental plane that he called overmind. He called the cosmic intelligence—that which governs the functioning of the universe—as supermind. He hypothesized that one can invoke the descent of supermind into one's self through the practice of *yoga*. He laid out a road map. That he called as integral *yoga*. There is no need to dissect or distinguish; *Raj Yoga* is the royal road.

OVERMIND

Sri Aurobindo's description of overmind almost connotes it to *turya*. There is self awareness. But perception is different. Words come to have a different semantics. Images become symbols and, they seem to come alive. There can be a dialogue with them!

One may internalize them. When that begins, *pratyahara* has happened. And ***Dharana*** begins.

MINDFULNESS IS A GATEWAY

A passive minding of the mind to prevent it from wandering, and, even from wondering as to what is *happening*, brings about a meditative state that we call mindfulness. Since, all kind of meditative practices finally go forward to a state of non-duality—*samadhi*; *pratyahara* may by itself produces enough by-products. This is validated with scientific investigation as seen before. Therefore, it is one of the most popular practices. Those who stay over here will also find a reduction in stress and, peace. For those who want to advance, there are only two more steps to attain *kaivalya*—an experience of *Thou art That*. It is bound to happen since that alone is the natural attribute of all human beings. It is a lone journey to Alone; *That only Is*. We shall further study the process now.

Chapter 8

Communion with Consciousness through the Realms of Over Mind

SUBSISTENCE AND DISSOLUTION AT SANCTUM SANCTORUM

Sri Aurobindo coined a new word, Over Mind. It connotes the domain beyond the usual functioning of the mind. It is a corridor connecting directly to the cosmic intelligence: Sri Aurobindo used the word Super Mind. Regardless of the linguistics, these domains of consciousness are not ordinary, mental functioning. Here we are entering the *sanctum sanctorum*—the inner most sacred space of the process in meditation.

So far we discussed a preparation that encompasses the outward expressions of the mind through behaviour. We reviewed how to get an entry to the subtle spheres of consciousness by shunning and shunting out the random thoughts. Before proceeding to the next steps, let us repeat, reinforce, and recapitulate as to what we have remembered. The practice makes a person perfect.

We have established a fundamental platform to advance in meditation. A paradigm shift of consciousness to the Fourth

State is the *sine qua non;* primary basis to proceed and progress further.

Here, the dialectical discussions cease. Meditation is a wholistic state of synchronous functioning of both the hemispheres of the brain. Pertinent questions have been asked; and, have been suitably answered. Discussion and debate have generated a comprehensive understanding. Thus, a debate is conducive to advancement of logical processing. But there cannot be endless debate. Rabindranath Tagore has sung; Let even my poetry be also mute! Grammar is not included in the process of meditation.

Summarizing, division into eight different steps for the process by Patanjali is conducive to the receptivity of analytical left brain functioning. That makes understanding easier. For experiencing *the* experience, dissection must now come to an end. Yet, the description has to follow in *seriatim.*

SUSTENANCE TO DERIVE SUBSISTENCE—*DHARANA*

By one estimate, during the course of a day, approximately 24,000 thoughts have a random play in the mind. This experiment has an inbuilt fallacy. The fact that every thought had to be registered by pressing a button to register account included a variable that would restrict the randomness of the thoughts. The ideation that we want to focus on a subject restricts the randomness in the mind. This is further enhanced by focusing—holding on, to a subject that is in synchrony with the sensibilities of the personality of the meditator.

The subject may be an abstract idea. Einstein has described his creative process as interplay with symbols in a state of reverie. To Sri Aurobindo the characters in the epic poem Savitri came alive in a virtual living state. The poem flowed with dialogue between them and the author as well.

QUINTESSENCE OF THE PROCESS: *DHYANA*

This takes us to the question: what should be meditated upon?

To answer this we take resort to a classical dictum.

Yada bhavah, tad bhavana;
Yada bhavana, tad bhavatu.

"What is intensely experienced in its totality, it transforms in to a feeling. What is extensively and wholistically felt in the entire being that materalises in to an actual form."

Meditation begins with processing psychodynamics; I am now beginning to meditate. We have already discussed mindfulness meditation and *vipassana*. They are aimed at cooling the mind to a state of calm and composed peaceful state. For most this by itself is enough. Progress beyond entails and encompasses a communion with cosmic consciousness. This is a journey beyond the realms of mental sphere. It involves an altogether different dimension: that we have not discussed so far. There are methods, as mentioned below, that connect to the cosmic consciousness.

PATTERNS AND METHODS

Since time immemorial, blessings and prayers were emphatically positive. *Rishis* of *Rig Veda* prayed so that good thoughts may come to them from all the sides. The meditation follows through the steps of focalisation on positive creative contents. The contents are portently pregnant with symbolic meaning. The techniques are multifarious.

Let us understand too commonly utilized methods. Invocation through recitation of a *mantra* of one's choice that may be a symbol of a deity, or a musical chant, signifying virtues may be taken as a vehicle.

Visualisation during meditation is a live experience. This may be of some aesthetic beauty of a panorama. It may be the performance of a ritual invocation with connotation to a particular merit. Or an icon may come alive. This, as per the belief of the meditator elicits a response with particular reference to the properties meditated upon.

Beyond this there are advanced techniques. They are in practice since ancient times. They are spiritually formatted. Apparently they seem to be intricate and at times, intriguing—mystical techniques. That is *tantra.* This is not within the ambit of the present study.

Advance techniques involve all the five senses. The elaboration progresses in numerous ways to either selectively advance a particular faculty or the totality of being.

DESTINATION TO THE DESTINY

We are about to know how to carve a certain future for ourselves. There is no room now for dialectical discussion about the veracity between freewill or a pre-ordained design to an individual or The Universe. We are the creator of our destiny. This happens through the intricate internalization of positive thoughts that generate positive actions through changes in the circuitry of neurons. There is a transformation of programme in the Unconscious. Neuroscientific explanation is, what is virtually experienced as a live phenomenon in trance, is further reflected by mirror imaging of the neurons. Neurons establish new connections as well as brain plasticity (*vide supra*, Chapter 5).

The hypothesis takes a quantum jump with addition of a significant parameter to the process. That is coming to a stage where psychodynamics has almost ceased: the thought has come to a single pointed awareness as a focal point. There is attention without any mental tension. There can be a minor disturbance; without digression. This quantum jump brings the consciousness to a different paradigm. A communion with the universal consciousness is now happening.

Let us have a pause before going forward.

CHOICELESS AWARENESS: OR AN ASPIRATION

For a select few, meditation by itself will be a spiritual pursuit without goal orientation. It is frequently described as choiceless awareness. Having had a quantum jump to connect with the universal natural cosmic forces, this is a way to synchronize oneself with the flow of Nature. It is a submission to the Unknown. There is no ambition. Desires have no place. The destination is towards the Unforeseen; and with complete disregard for a wish to see it. This is indeed rare.

To wish for a state of desirelessness is also a desire. A recluse may choose randomness. For most of us, we want to set some goals and want to have a direction. This kind of aspiration is not a digression from spirituality. Aspirations may be a divine inspiration.

Guru

For those who are inclined to accept a *guru*, and are fortunate to find one, this will be a well charted path. A *guru* is an adept, who has intrinsic intuitive, understanding of the sensibilities and personality type of the follower. He is totally unselfish. His motivation to guide is inspired by compassionate kindness. He wishes to part with his intuitive wisdom. Needles to say, his motivation to guide will only be to point a finger towards *the* way. He has to be purely spiritual. He can never dominate. He must not dictate. Most *gurus* have treaded and traded on a structured format. This has yielded for them the desired objectives.

Therefore, it will be appropriate to follow a method that has provided evidence for its efficacy. Contradictions may arise out of cultural conflicts. The *guru* may demand a ritualistic initiation. It is left to the sensibilities and the belief systems of the follower.

Beware of a commercial *guru*. Spirituality evaporates at the touch of commerce.

WAY, PATH, METHODS AND ROADMAPS

There are innumerable methods. The formats vary. There are voluminous explorations on the semantics. We simplify as follows:

What is experienced with a background of profound feelings gets deeply engraved in all the layers of the mind. This keeps on surfacing on to the character and personality of the individual and also reflects on to the behaviour. With constant itineration of the practice, repetition reinforces the pursuit towards a desired goal. That certainly fructifies over a period of time. This achievement is individually designed and consigned for the meditator as per the methodology that he/she has adopted.

The process will now progress to the advance and deeper state of *turya*. It may be like the smooth, quite flow of a river. Or there may be piloting a flight across the fifth and sixth state of consciousness (*vide supra*, ch. 1) to cosmic consciousness. That will be an experience of non-duality that we will see later.

There are inexplicable phenomena that come to *happen*. Patanjali described them as unravelling of eight paranormal faculties. They are:

1. *Anima*: ability to see the minute of the minutest.
2. *Mahima*: ability to perceive with large and wholistic view.
3. *Laghima*: ability to be lighter in weight.
4. *Garima*: ability to make oneself very heavy.

These qualities made a subject of intensive investigation into occult phenomena. This was fanciful and mystic. Madame Blavatsky and Colonel Alcott traveled to India to learn occult secrets from Swami Dayananda. To their dismay, Swami told them that he knows none of that! Annie Besant and Leadbeater pursued them to discover amazing facts about the subatomic structure unknown at that time. They deserve mention since it is a fantastic achievement beyond fantasy (Refer Table 5.2, *vide Supra*).

A further elaboration from even the medieval times is in Jain philosophy (Refer Table 5.3, *vide Supra*).

Let us revert to modern times. Herbert Benson was lead to the Dalai Lama to discover a faculty amongst the Buddhist meditators; they could warm up the body at will. It was said that they may even levitate. They failed to do so. Maharshi Mahesh Yogi drew large audiences with his pronouncements for levitation with TM practice. Only Jefferson, as mentioned earlier, could do so.

For the present day the pursuit of any occult practice is out of order. Science of the present sanctuary has made sophisticated equipment available to investigate Nature and its numerous manifestations. Therefore, we leave the occult only for the record and discuss what is of relevance to the present time.

FACULTIES WITH RELEVANCE TO MODERNITY

The relevant faculties are:

1. *Prapti:* a spontaneous revelation of hidden, inherent faculties to human beings such as clairvoyance, clairaudience, prophecy, time regression, time progression and time undulation. This happens in synchrony with achieving a desired destination.
2. *Prakamya*: to arrive at total fulfilment for all that is worthy to be desired.
3. *Ishita:* to generate a creative power with capabilities to bring physical, actual formatting as if in real life; with communion to cosmic consciousness.

4. *Vashita:* is the faculty to control others' mind as well as the environment that may include the Nature.

VISTARS BEYOND THE REALM OF MIND

An enquirer may still ask for further explanation. A plausible explanation may be a well defined Neuroscientific phenomenon. Most of us are familiar with the tricks that a monkey plays. A monkey can instantly replay what he sees. Focalisation on any noble thought, aesthetic panorama or, an icon with specific virtues; or silent recitation in the mind of a *mantra* with specific invocation, is bound to generate peace, tranquillity and serenity. This happens since there is firing of parallel neurons. Focalisation on a single point by itself will slow down the flow of thoughts in mind. This saves mental energy. That gets chanelized so as towards enhancement of creativity as one of the non-specific natural accrual of faculties discussed above. The methods to meditate abound from utterly simplistic to highly sophisticated. We begin with a simple method enunciated by Swami Satyananda.

YOGA NIDRA: BIHAR SCHOOL

Swami Satyananda utterly simplified *Raj Yoga* practice. It was meant for everybody. He utilized the posture of lying down on a non-conductor of electricity. Then one was to start commanding parts of the body one by one; say begin with the toe of right foot. All the muscles of the right foot were commanded with a conscious focalized thought to relax. When this proceeded from toe to the head of the right side, the entire right half of the body was perceived as limp. The contrast between the right and the left was now observed. And, the left was similarly ordered to feel as relaxed as the other one; and, go limp. Thus, there was progressive muscular relaxation all over the body. He utilized the hypothesis that with a relaxed body, a tense mind must also relax. The subject usually had a nap or a sleep like state for a few minutes.

This simple technique has its basis in the *Hath Yoga* practice of *Shavasana*. It correlates with a similar primary form of Buddhist meditation: meditation on body awareness. Surprisingly, it may seem, Earnest Hemmingway won a Nobel price for his book *The Old Man and the Sea*! The book was a monologue between the single character—'Old Man', and his body parts.

Swami Satyananda taught as below:

Welcome to *Yoga Nidra* session. Now let us warm up for *Yoga Nidra*. I lie down on my back in *Shavasana*. I cover myself with the bed sheet. My spine and head are in a straight line, with palms and the hands facing upwards and legs slightly apart. I make myself completely comfortable. Feel a sense of settling down. I close my eyes slowly and gently. Ensure that there is no stiffness or tense feeling in any part of the body.

Let us understand what *Yoga Nidra* is. It is a systematic practice for achieving total physical, mental and emotional relaxation simultaneously. It is gathering of total energy at a point in the mind. *Yoga Nidra* can be practiced generally at any time of the day by any one, but in particular, before going to bed.

I follow the instructions without any reservation in my mind or any diversion either by way of speaking or debating with my self. Relax my mind to become calm and quite. Do not have any thought except of relaxation of my body and mind. There must not be any physical movements, just as I do before going to sleep. I remember that this is not sleep. I am mentally alert and aware without any rigidity in the mind and body. As I closely observe my body, my mind is moving into a new realm of my consciousness. Simply listen the words and follow.

I resolve in my mind with faith in the God of my choice. I repeat my resolve thrice, slowly, clearly without making any sound. Now visualize the *yoga* hall from outside. I enter the hall and visualize its ceilings, walls, windows, floor, carpet and also the space around my body. I look at my body. It is lying on the floor motionless. I see from head to toe and again from toe to head. *Yoga Nidra* is bringing me to a total physical and mental balance. I am aware of the consciousness within me. I am now feeling the energy flowing through my body and completely from point to point.

Now I am becoming aware of my right hand, right thumb, ring finger, middle finger, index finger and the little singer. I feel the tips of the fingers. I am aware of my palms, the wrist, the elbow, the shoulders, the arm-pit, the right side of the trunk, the right thigh, the knee cap, the calf muscle, the ankle, the heel, the sole. Become aware of your right sole, the right foot, the right big toe, second toe, third toe, fourth toe and the fifth toe. Now I am aware of the left side the same way of the left side. Now I am becoming aware of the top of the head, both sides of the forehead, the right and left eye brow, the space between the eye brows. I feel this particular psychic centre very deeply. I become aware of the right and left ear, the right and left cheek, the nose, the tip of the nose, the upper and lower lip, the chin, the throat, the right and left chest, the middle of the Chest, the naval and the abdomen.

Now I am aware of my back. I am aware of the right and left shoulder blade, the right buttock and left buttock. Now I stress my consciousness upon my spine from lower end to upper end and then over the whole of the back.

Now the awareness is pervading all the parts of the body, whole of right leg, whole of left leg, both legs together, whole of right arm, whole of left arm, both arms together, whole of the back, buttocks, spine, whole of the front of abdomen, chest and the whole of the face.

The whole of the head and body together is lying totally relaxed on the floor. My body is lying perfectly still on the floor in this room.

Now I become aware of my natural breathing. I am breathing in and out. I feel the flow of air in and out of my lungs … the rhythm of my breathing is natural, automatic. Now I am looking on the movements of my navel. It is rising and falling with every breath. Now I start counting my breathing from 21 to 0. Breathe in first keeping in mind the number 21 and breathe out keeping in mind the same number. Repeat this exercise every time diminishing the number by 1 till you reach zero. If I make a mistake, I go back to 21 and start all over again…. Do not miss a single count…. I am counting the breaths with my entire attention. I don't go to sleep … now, leave the counting at whatever the number you are and detach your awareness from your breathing.

Now I am recollecting the experience of pain. Any kind of pain I have experienced in my life, I am remembering it; I feel that pain … yes, that pain has come alive as of now. I touch the pain, the painful part of my body with my hand that are as cold as ice….I press the ice to the painful part. The pain has frozen. It is now…It is gone.

I am now experiencing the feeling of pleasure, joy, happiness; Ananda ….the joyful event is coming alive. I see it vividly happening with the totality surrounding the event… The people, the friend, the flavours and the ambience around … I see even the guardian angels….I sense their perfume, what a fragrance that is !!! The ambience of the event, the joy and delight has pervaded in and around the whole body!!!

I am taking the ambience of this experience in totality now to the present date.

Just feel a calm and quiet early morning. I am walking by the side of the bank of the river with clean and transparent water, both sides of the river are green, cool breeze is kissing my face. The morning is splendid and beautiful, the birds are singing and now … I am alone walking away from all the noise of the city.

Now I am seeing the sun rise. It is like a crimson red ball, gradually coming up. Now I am feeling the divine pink rays emerging from the sun. They are entering into each and every part my body. My whole body is being merged in the divine light of pink rays. I am walking near a small place of worship on the bank. Now I am moving inside the temple … very calm … sitting softly there… with closed eyes, meditating deeply … merging my consciousness with the super consciousness.

I am in complete solitude and tranquillity: inner bliss is flowing within me… I resolve the resolution that I made at the beginning that remains with me for ever. I resolve thrice with full awareness and strength … Gently I come back from the inner journey to the surface again, back to my body. I become aware of my natural breathing.

I feel wide awake. I gently turn to the side, taking my own time, without hurry and slowly I sit up calmly. I open my eyes. The *Yoga Nidra* has ended.

ADVANCE FORMULATION OF RAJ YOGA: KASHMIR SCHOOL

Advaita—non-dual-philosophy flourished in Kashmir. It culminated into the worship of *Siva*. Here, *Siva* connotes the cosmos. The immutable *Siva* manifests through the medium of *Sakti*. An individual is seen as a fragment from the composite whole: that incorporates *Siva* and *Sakti* both. The philosophy translated to numerous forms of meditation. We study the essence.

Pandits from Kashmir developed several thousands of methods to meditate. They were based on a fundamental philosophical postulate that *Siva*—to be understood as representing cosmic consciousness. It is the primary source of origin of the Universe. What was before the beginning is unknown. But, intelligence came first. All the universal manifestations arose from cosmic consciousness. This intelligence manifests as Nature. Thus, the material manifestation exists with the transformation of cosmic energy into physical forms. An individual lives most of the time with an illusion that he/she is an independent self-content entity. *Raj Yoga* is a method whereby the fragmented energy portion finds the reunion with its creative source—cosmic consciousness. Fundamental postulate of this school is energy as a primary source. Validation with scientific bases is on the principal that energy is indestructible; it can transform from one form to another. An energy and matter are inter-convertible.

Kashmir School describes the method as follows:

The initial step initiated by the Kashmir School requires affirmation and unconditional acceptance of above. The *gurus* of this School are getting fewer.

Initiation of the process of the reunion of individual consciousness to cosmic consciousness begins with a resolve to evolve the ordinary everyday consciousness engaged in mundane activities to a higher state of quest. The quest is to fathom the heights and depths of cosmic consciousness. The quest can certainly fructify by deploying the energy in such a way that (1) There is no wastage of energy after wounding matters. (2) The energy is chanelized towards the aspired goal. (3) A source of creating a fresh energy is discovered within the physical body.

The individual consciousness extends to transcendental realms. There is expansion to extensive awareness that the universe is a manifestation of cosmic energy. The course to the refined method of *Raj Yoga* to create rejuvenating energy and invoking the divine grace leads to the transcendental consciousness. The experience of joyful state—*Anand* now persists all the while.

Such a state brings about a paradigm shift. Ego, as I—the doer dissolves. The individual now persists himself as an instrument of divine. Paranormal faculties spontaneously reveal themselves. Aspiration may arise in the state of transcendental consciousness (*turya* and beyond). It needs to be emphasized here that the desires in the mental plane must not be mistaken for aspiration.

The aspirations express themselves as intuitive insight. They are a foresight into the future. This may be easily acceptable for those with faith in the divine design. Neuroscience and Quantum Physics of this process is yet obscure. Regardless, aspiration does actualize. So alternatively, the happening may be attributed to the formative power of cosmic energy that was imbibed by the meditator. There is reflection of the delightful joy to the surrounding as well.

Energized by the cosmic energy, the subtle and sublime experiences can create a (w)holistic perception of fragmented reality. There can be critical analytical understanding of a complex situation. Physical expression may also be exquisite, such as expansion of electro-magnetic field, healing from a disorder to an ordinary stage etc. A meditator imbibes energy in various forms. Different forms of energy transforms into different formats. One of the formats may be a *mantra*. This is left to the particular sensibilities of the personality of the meditator. With profound faith derived from ancient Pandit of Kashmir, we now move on to discover how to imbibe cosmic energy. A well established vehicle is a *mantra*. Transcendental meditation (TM) technique is derived mainly from Patanjali. The *mantras* in TM technique have origins from Kashmir School.

Thus, a *mantra* is selected on two basic principles. Its known verbal recitation in the mind is supposed to generate a specific kind of quality. This quality, with regular daily practices will enhance a qualitative merit to the personality of the mediator. The other point for relevance of selecting a particular *mantra* is the sensibility of the person. The *gurus* derive these *mantras* from ancient texts. Selection is with the faith of the meditator. The *mantra* helps to steady the mind. From this focal point, the state of *turya* may begin; or enhance.

We elaborate on a few *mantras.*

Aum, a composite of three letters, A, U, M is primordial. It is the first sound that ever was heard before anything that existed. It is reverberating through the entire universe. With faith established firmly into this belief, the *mantra* establishes unity with the universe. The universe and the cosmos were one; at the source. The apparent division is a delusion. Reconnection at the source creates harmony.

Gayatri Mantra is a celebrated worship of the sun.

> *Aum bhur bhuva svaha, tatsa vitur varanya;*
> *Bhargo devasya dhi mahi, dhiyo yo nah pracho dayat.*

It translates as:

> That sun full of effulgence which illumines all the worlds, may shine upon our intellect to make it brilliant. This *mantra* is a creative source of abundant energy. It also sharpens the intelligence. When recited together with visualization of a rising sun, full of shining splendour, and should be incorporated in the self. This will be conducive to generate a personality whose presence is immediately felt.

OM MANI PADME HUM

This is a universal Buddhist *mantra* that will be discussed later.

Purity must be achieved by an indivisible unity of method and wisdom, symbolized by the final word, *hum*. In the *mantra* it refers to one consciousness in which there is full form of both, wisdom and method. So, that two cannot be differentiated and become a single entity. *Hum* is the seed syllable of *Akshobhya*—immovable, the non-fluctuating, that which cannot be disturbed by anything.

Summarizing an apparent meaningless word would steady the mind. Experimenting with non-verbal chanting of 1, 2, 3 may not even generate a trance state. Instead it may produce boredom. With the faith that the numbers are conative of a symbolic non-variant truth that does not change with time and place, will infuse the insight into mathematics. Thus, meditation primarily begins as a process in the mind of the meditator and it has hardly anything to do with a particular method.

The renewed and regenerated energy dissolves egocentric personality. Simultaneously, there is diminution of various neurotic tendencies of the personality. Subtle realms of individual consciousness are far beyond the physical body come to be realized. A *mantra* may be symbolic of a feminine deity signifying energy form; say, *Durga*. Such a meditation brings into action, the formative power so that evil is destroyed and there is victory of all that is virtuous.

A word of caution is mandatory here. An outburst of profound energy may skip a fit of the meditator from ground reality. It may be like pouring off molten metal in glassware. A frequent occurrence, inspite there being a mentor is apparent sexual behaviour.

In summary, no two human beings are alike. Each individual has a distinctively personal identity. However, his/her consciousness is artificially fragmented form of cosmic whole. Forces of nature control him/her conversely the reverse also does happen.

According to Kashmir School, meditation with a *mantra* is complex. In state of *dhyana*, it is postulated that the meditator and the *mantra* becomes one. A particular *mantra* will thus have a specific outcome. Therefore, initiation and mentoring by a guru becomes significant. The *mantra* may connote a particular deity. Let this not be mistaken for icon worship. The deity is chosen according to form of the virtues that it symbolizes. Kashmir School has expounded in depth how a mantra is formulated. Suffice it may to understand that phonetics and resonance of all the *mantras* lead the meditator to the identity and union with cosmic consciousness.

KUNDALINI AND *CHAKRAS*

The process is highly mystic. The energy that is needed for this evolution arises from a *mantra*. At the onset, there is awakening of a hypothetical coiled up serpentile energy—*Kundalini* at the root of the spinal cord. This energy moves upward through various *chakras* (Figure 8.1). Anatomically, *chakras* are networks of nerve plexuses that regulate body function autonomously. The energy is visualized as moving upwards from the root of spinal cord to the crown of the head, traversing seven *chakras* on its way (Figure 8.1). In conclusion, there is profound philosophy and highly mystic techniques in Kashmir School. It is focused on *Siva* as a source to the origin of cosmos. It ends with the union by the practitioner to the source. This is mistakenly considered as *Siva* worship.

TM meditation formulated *mantras* without specific meaning. It was said that there was divine divination by rishis. The *rishis* heard the sound from the sky and a *mantra* was born. Initiation into TM was available to all at a minimal fee. The authors are privileged to have been initiated at the *ashram* in Rishikesh before 40 years. They remain practicing the method with several modifications. This invoked the symbolic, implied

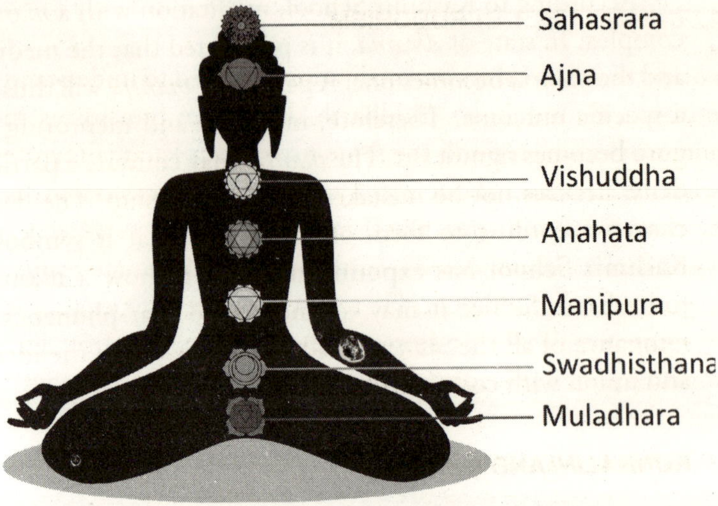

Fig. 8.1: Seven Chakras: Transcendental Meditation: Rishikesh and MERU (Maharshi European Research University)

meaning to the *sutras*. Several *sutras* were to be focused with mindful meditation on their symbolic significance. Maharshi Mahesh Yogi termed it as *siddhi* programme. This advancement was aimed at fructification of special faculties for the achievement of a desired result.

One of the greatest achievements of this movement was to assemble 7,000 accomplished meditators at one place. Number 7,000 was derived with some intricate mathematical formula that would be significant for the total population of the world at that time. The assembly meditated for a few days. Maharshi published the data of this experiment that claimed to have significantly affected the social coherence.

TM movement has slowed down and almost faded after the demise of Maharshi. *Meru* survives and initiates at Seelisberg in Switzerland.

VAJRAYANA TIBETAN BUDDHISM

To orient towards *Vajrayana* meditation, we need to understand the origin of Buddhism. Siddharth the Prince transforms to Gautama Buddha around the same time when Patanjali wrote his Master Treatise. About 2500 years ago, Prince Siddhartha sat under the Bodhi tree practising severe penance. After 42 days of fasting, he pondered over the nature of ultimate reality. He attained enlightenment. He realized that severe penance is not a prerequisite to understand the Ultimate Reality. The Ultimate Nature of Reality manifested to him as *sunyata* (void). While the universe has a beginning and end in the very nature of *sunyata*, all the phenomena come to be derived from it. That way, all the occurrences are interconnected and therefore, interdependent. An individual is also a natural phenomenon, therefore, all such occurrences all over the globe, are connected wholistically. This deductive logic, though easily understood by ordinarily intelligent persons, is not easily realized so that one can derive virtues from it. One has to change the paradigm from the discursive logic to an experience that can be generated only after an initiation.

The initiation leads to the gateways of *Vajrayana*, The *Vajrayana* practice has pacified innumerable minds, drawn numerous pupils to Buddhism and generated controversies! For every Buddhist, a logical understanding of the philosophical precepts is not enough. Buddhists are trained in dialectics so as to intelligently appreciate philosophy. However, the discursive thought bifurcated into two main streams. *Hinyana* Buddhism advocated *sadhana* towards the attainment of *nirvana* for oneself, so as to be liberated from the cyclic existence. *Mahayana* postulated that there are several layers of attainment. The one who has progressed higher should revert back so that he takes along the less enlightened with him. One should therefore, of necessity strive to lessen the suffering of all fellow beings.

Buddha also came to realize that the Ultimate Reality could be deduced by understanding the basis of suffering and methods to alleviate them. But this pondering was not dialectical discursive play of thought. Instead, it was in the nature of inner reflection and contemplation. This process, which begins in the mind and leads one to go beyond mind, is what we call meditation today. Through the meditative process, Buddha came to understand the Four Noble Truths. He also came to know the real nature of suffering. Suffering is real; there must be a cause to the suffering. When the cause of suffering is discovered, it can be removed. From such simple logical basics, Ashwaghosh and Nagarjuna expounded a profound Buddhist philosophy. This turned into a religion, Buddhism. Buddhism is atheist. Yet, the icon worship abounds. Each individual is a potential Buddha. And there is a feminine form, *Tara—Sakti*. All positive thoughts and spiritual qualities find their form in a particular Buddha. These are available as paintings across the globe. That has: The simplicity of the philosophy, atheism and universal spiritual virtues have made Buddhism popular. In the 8th century, a Buddhist monk Paramsambhava crossed the Himalayas to convert the king, and the almost entire marshal Tibetan race to Buddhism.

We begin with a universal Buddhist *mantra*:

OM MANI PADME HUM

We have already understood the significance of this *mantra* (*vide supra*). Purity must be achieved by an indivisible unity of method and wisdom, symbolized by the final word, *hum*. In the *mantra* it refers to one consciousness in which there is full form of both, wisdom and method. So, that two cannot be differentiated and become a single entity. *Hum* is the seed syllable of *Akshobhya Buddha*—immovable, the non-fluctuating, that which cannot be disturbed by anything.

The visualized techniques are refined in Buddhist *Vajrayana* echnique.

Buddhist *Vajrayana* meditation adds visualization of specific orms of Buddhas. The meditative techniques arising out of the arious forms of Buddha are easy to practice. They yield relevant esults. There are several different kinds of Buddhas with specific ualities. *Avalokiteshwar Buddha* symbolizes compassion. The neditation on that generates a compassionate kind generosity. *mitabh Buddha* symbolizes wisdom. That generates critical, nalytical, dialectical and logical thinking. *Rittasambhava uddha* stands for valour and adventure. Meditating on this uddha will enhance quick action with foresight and sharpness n action. *Amogha-Siddhi Buddha* leads the path to ccomplishment of all that is possible with human and uperhuman abilities. It leads the path towards the realization f *Sunyata*; the ultimate Void, absolute emptiness that is the rigin of all creation. Addition of a feminine form of *Tara* gnifies all pervading cosmic energy. While anyone of the name rms may be focalized on to in meditation. It can be advanced y successive transition from one form to all the five forms. he cycle repeats itself. This is cyclic meditation. This is ructured as *Ghuyha Samaj Tantra.* Faith in the Buddhist ostulates is a necessary prerequisite. The empowerment ensues ith confirmation of the Buddhist postulates and an express ish to take refuge in *Dharma.*

Vajrayana is full of techniques-*tantra*—that can lead to the tainment of desired goals. Its practice generates *Bodhichitta*, a ure state of consciousness. Further, it leads one to a state of *odhisattva*. A *Bodhisattva* reincarnates at will. This is for the tterment of the fellow beings. The reincarnation is self invited om the compassionate kindness to alleviate the sufferings of e sentient beings on the earth. For the attainment of such an complishment *Vajrayana* practices are a must; needless to say at it cannot be for one and all.

The Dalai Lama is one such *Bodhisattva*. It is, therefore, that he repeatedly sings,

> "As long as suffering lasts, and misery exists in this world; I shall be born again and again, to alleviate the suffering of my fellow beings."

GUHAYA SAMAJ SADHANA: MEDITATION FOR IN-DEPTH WISDOM

For all kinds of initiations, one has to leave one's ego, Interconnectedness and interdependence are appreciated only thorough a realization that no man is an island. So he has to take help from the enlightened ones, from recourse to *dharma*, and seeking refuge in the collective consciousness/wisdom of the group. In *Guhyasa Samaj sadhana*, this is the first step. It is recited as an experience in the inner mind as:

> "I go for refuge continually to the Buddhas in whose mind abides ament play (realization of void) actualized in stages like the waxing of the stainless moon and infinite methods of pure compassion."

> "I go for refuge continually to the holy *Dharma*. This is the basis for total freedom from all misconceptions and, the foundation for the excellence of the holy beings."

> "I go for refuge to the *gurus*, *Bodhisattvas*, who are masters of discipline abide on the stages of progress. The masters are endowed with a glory of *Bodhi*. This is incited by supreme compassion. They became freed from the setter they progressed."

And following such a surrendering of will, there is a resolve that, "I shall generate my mind into a pure *Bodhichitta*. This will be adorned with a pure selfless wish." Having arrived at a state of complete relaxation and having thrown all the worries to the wind, there is intense creative visualization. This is visualizing various forms of Buddha as well the feminine deity Tara. And one has to imbibe the qualitative virtues of these deities.

Further empowerment is derived by chanting of *HUM* and various other *sutras*. Before concluding, one takes refuge into Buddhas, such as *Akshobhya Vajra, Vairochana, Ratnasambhava, Vajra Amitabha* and *Amoghasiddhi Vajra*. (*Vide supra*).

The visualization ends by a resolve when one sees that "by virtue of meditation, may I swiftly attain the state of *Vajradhara*—it connotes an entire conglomeration of Buddhas. It is (w)holistic so as to incorporate the nature of all the Buddhas. May I practice both kinds of activities, those actions that are for becoming enlightened, as well as those being of a fully Enlightened Buddha. May there be no interference to my proper attainment. And by spreading and causing it to flourish in all directions, space and times, may I free all beings by this skilful means.

The Dalai Lama initiated the authors in *Ghuyha Samaj Tantra* as follows:

Buddhist meditation centres are spread across the globe. Mindfulness, the simplest Buddhist technique is taught at the universities. A simple technique satisfies the need and motivation of the most, towards a peaceful, harmonious, stress free life. A few have high aspirations. For them the ultimate form of Buddhist meditation is *Kalachakra* initiation. This is ritualistic, involves taking vow; but does not need a change of robe to being a monk.

ADDITIONAL TIBETAN BUDDHIST MEDITATIVE PRACTICES

Meditation on Meta, Compassion

The well-charted path begins from the common ground that pertains to all of us. Almost all of us know what it is to suffer. Having known the pain for oneself, it is but natural for empathy to ensue for those who are suffering. The recommended first step is to meditate on Meta, i.e. compassion. The beginner is advised to appreciate how much his life depended upon the kindness of others. Even then compassion may not arise of its own. This universal love is not the customary/habitual attitude of the mind. It must be cultivated. The cultivation is easy to begin firstly with oneself. A person finds no difficulty to reflect upon how ones own well-being has to be looked after. It should then follow that the others also have the same desires and are equally entitled to happiness.

Meditation on Meta is aimed at the liberation of the mind from hatred, ill will, anger and selfishness. In the beginning the meditator affirms his self-love, viz. that is his own concern for freedom from the enmity. It soon leads to the understanding that the others also have the same concern for their own well-being. So it is natural to wish them their well-being and happiness. Then he extends his love to those who are his family members and friends, Then to the neutral people and then even to those who are his enemies or for whom he has hostile feelings.

When the aversion is experienced, one reflects on the law of cause and effect, or the karmic connection. There may have been such connection in the past that the enemy is hostile to him. It may be possible to know or it is lost in the past. But the karmic connection is operative all the time. An act of aversion, hostility or enmity now to the hated person would bring out harm in two ways; it will breed further enmity and, even before that the negative feelings will do self-damage.

The Dalai Lama's advice is to begin by reflecting on the selfless love of a mother. Imagine the motherhood prevalent in all beings in nature and take it further to the thought that all of them could be your mothers. But such altruistic activities, though admired by the most, may not be practicable by all. The Tibetan Buddhist practices have a recipe of the most varied variety. It is said that there are at least a few thousand methods to practice meditation and one can choose to suit one's own disposition. For those who are inclined to be rational and analytical, *vipassyana* is a good method to begin.

Samata Meditation

There are other methods, and a teacher may facilitate the choice after knowing one's disposition. Torn as we are in the modern civilization by the pulls of opposites, another common offering is Samata meditation. This teaches equipoise and is again based on the standard precepts of dependent origination that guides to the ultimate realization of *sunyata*.

Meditation to Generate Bodhichitta

A *bodhichitta* has evolved to a state where manipulations by the mind are cast away. He functions in the society. But his actions are not egocentric: he is guided by the comprehensive good of the society. Therefore, this meditation encompasses all such virtues as compassion, equanimity etc. as discussed above. The result is a perception that is devoid of any neurosis. The method is suitable even for beginners. After practicing mindfulness for sometime, it will be easier. Having begun to meditate, the experience of the fourth state of consciousness is enough of an incentive to enhance aspiration.

Self reflection begins with experience of *Turia*. That will have cultivated to leave behind the coarse mind. One has then to progress to a single pointed method of once own choice; or simply focus on a dot (*Bindu*). There can be a silent recitation of a mantra, say *Om Mani Padme Hum.* This will lead to a direct intuitive experience of sunyata. No sooner we have understood the nature of *sunyata* even at the cognitive level. There is a quantum jump to the penultimate. This generates an aspiration for *bodhichitta*—a compassionate wish to attain Buddhahood for the benefit of others.

The practices we discussed so far belong to Mahayana tradition. They are helpful in eliminating the agitation of the coarse mind. One can be a guide to one's own path so far. The *Vajrayana* practices are very sophisticated and profound in meaning. The core of the method is to focus single pointedly at one or more images. The image can be a pebble, a piece of wood or any other object on your study table. It could preferably be an image of a deity—may be Christ or any other symbolic image according to one's belief. But this should not be equated with image worship. The images of the deities are symbolic in content; say *Avalokiteshwara* Buddha connotes the virtue of compassion, *Amitabh* Buddha connotes the merit of wisdom, or for that matter, *Tara* symbolizes the energy and might. Either a single image may be preferred or there can be many as per the method. Instead of, or in addition to, there can be a silent recitation of a mantra, say

KALACHAKRA INITIATION

Kalachakra meditation is the highest form of *Vajrayana* initiation. In the entire Tibetan tradition the Dalai Lama and only a few others are entitled to give this initiation. Initiation is like the empowerment ceremony—the inauguration of an elected person to an office. He has to be worthy of it by first acquiring merit and when thought suitable, he/she is given initiation. The ceremony lasts about a week. An elaborate *mandala* is prepared with the symbolic deities located inside. *Kalachakra mandala* has 928 images to meditate upon in rapid succession, imbibing the virtue of each symbol within oneself in the process of meditation. Such practice is only for highly advanced seekers. Special appeal of Buddhist meditation to the universal audience lies in the fact that the practices range from the elementary to the ultimate. This we have reviewed earlier.

The essence of the *Vajrayana path* is that it combines method and wisdom in the most impeccable way. This is so because a virtue or merit is initially attributed to the symbol, that is internalized and at the end of the meditation, it is dissolved into all pervading emptiness. This is generative of the subtle mind that gives the glimpse of the Fifth Dimension.

In conclusion, the distress ceases and the person stays in eustress. Most people are content with functionality in this way.

PO-WA MEDITATION: REFLECTION ON DEATH

Relevant to our discussion on consciousness is the method called *po-wa* visualizations in preparation for death.

A practitioner may say himself thus:

I have received teachings on the principal paths. I have meditated on them. I have received *Vajrayana* instructions and tried to practice them faithfully. But I have discovered that it is not possible for me to attain enlightenment in this life...so I intend to practice *po-wa* (literally translates as, transference of consciousness) to Amitabh's pure land. When the time of death comes, one transfers very subtle energy together with very subtle mind to the central channel of the spinal cord up to the crown of the head and out from there into Amitabh's pure land.

The exact steps of the practice are to visualize the central channel that should be seen as closer to the back, a little bit in front of spine. The channel is closed at the bottom but open at the crown of the head. Then the fundamental energy of the seed—syllable, i.e. *tig-le*—a Tibetan word meaning The Soul, is seen sitting like a small pea within the central channel at the level of the heart. Then make attempt to move the seed—syllable up and down the central channel. The seed syllable is brought to the level of the crown where the central channel is open. From the vantage point of the opening of the central channel, an attempt is made to look inside the channel. Go up and down the channel and see you cleaning up its interior.

Now visualize Amitabh Buddha seated in space in front of you at the level of the forehead. He is ruby red in colour and his entire body is made out of transparent radiant light. See yourself take refuge in the Amitabha and then see the radiant light energy coming from him down into the central channel. See it purifying you completely of all the hindrances. By means of such purification see the body slowly transform from gross physical to that of radiant light.

Now see the seed-syllable transforming itself. It is white in colour, clear as crystal with a slight reddish tint. It has become now a small radiant point of light, tiny vibrating star. Move it up and down the channel. Clean up all the *chakras* as it moves up and down the channel.

Breathe in deeply and at the same time tighten the lower muscles slightly at the level of the bottom of the body. Thus when the energy from the intake of your breath meets the tightened up energy from your bottom muscles, it makes you feel a blissful feeling. When you have done this for a few times and your blissful state intensifies, let go of the feeling all-together. It gives you a practice to give up something intensely pleasurable.

Now visualize the channel in front of you. Choose a dimension that is convenient. But it is seen open at the top like a lotus flower. And when you go to sleep tonight, see yourself going to the pure land of Amitabh through the opening at the top. Having learnt this technique, it will be possible to let go your subtle, very subtle level of mind out of the open central channel and take rebirth according to your wish.

Where does such meditative practice lead us? Without reinforcing the concept of the subtle mind, it is not easy to see the inherently non-existent, ever changing from moment to moment, only a conceptually designated, mere self. It has the functions as the other physical implements do. But that is not the *real self*. The real self is the subtle mind, the consciousness that is without a beginning and without an end. The dissolution in *nirvana* is there but it is neither beginning nor end. If the non-reality of the conceptual mere self is realized, then only one will be able to appreciate that even though, the essence of life, i.e. *tig-le* is said to be located in the heart. In a heart transplanted person it makes no difference when he performs *po-wa* meditation.

Reverting to the common parlance most people believe death is an event that happens to someone else. And that is not a delusion. As long as one exists, there is no death. When there is death, one doesn't exist. Yet, death is inevitable for all. Such a reflection generates insight about the impermanence of all phenomena. What happens after death? For most of us the question draws a blank. This can lead to the realization that existence by itself may be devoid of any substance. So, let there be peace!

CAUTION!

A word of caution about *Vajrayana* practice is needed. These are highly evolved techniques beyond mind, to put it very mildly. They cannot be undertaken without full preparation, initiation and supervision. Wondering, wandering, meandering through the meditative path in the Himalayas, Steve Jobs put the whole world of information on the finger tips of the entire mankind. Such an instant is a rarity. Several others discovered a way to live in peace and harmony. However, as an infrequent event may occur for some individuals. They might get skewed up and loose mental balance. They should avoid advance methods and, be content with simpler techniques like *Yoga Nidra* or mindfulness. Sometimes most extraordinary events happen.

The discussion on the methods can extend to further elaboration. The central theme of Kashmir School is *Siva*, and his manifest form, *Sakti*. Pandits of Kashmir have sculpted about 65,000 methods from ancient times! *Vajrayana*, having one single Buddha for a particular merit has also many more methods. Monasteries teach a particular method as per their time tested method. The worship of Vishnu is all across the Indian continent. And, Vishnu has 1,000 names: so also is the case with Lakshmi and Lalita. We need not further discuss any of these merits. There is rainfall on various geographically defined areas on the earth; it flows into rivers that are named differently. Final destination of all the rivers is one single ocean. And yet, in spite of oceans being confluent they are named differently.

GANAPATI FESTIVAL: A SYMBOLIC METAPHOR

The profound philosophical exposition of the postulates is aptly circumscribed as a ritualistic celebration. Ganapati festival is a symbolic metaphor of the last three steps of the meditative process. Beginning from his vehicle, a mouse, this elephantine God controls the mouse with a single toe. Metaphorically, the mouse represents the mind. Mind is the vehicle through which we all function. The characteristic of the mind and the mouse is to go from here to there and everywhere. Only when the mind is controlled, and prevented from wandering functionality can come into play. And yet a vehicle is necessary for the travel.

All the faculties that are represented by Ganesha can function in space and time through the facilitation by the mind.

Ganapati is sitting happily in a repose. There is a smile on his face. He has a large abdomen. That represents satiety. It also connotes that he has incorporated a huge amount of knowledge. That is being digested as wisdom. He has four arms. Each arm represents a distinct faculty. There is a lotus in one hand that is symbolic of refined aesthetics. As a contrast he has a weapon on the opposite side. Thus, the beauty is counterbalanced with valor. While he is gifting a sweet, the opposite hand is lifted up: blessings override any other kind of gift. Elephant is a symbol of wisdom; his elephantine head is symbolic of wisdom. The large ears are the receptacles for listening from all the sides. His slanting eyes seem to be looking not only in front but backwards as well. Ganesha has two consorts. They should also be understood as a metaphor. *Riddhi* signifies abundant wealth. *Siddhi* is the faculty for success. By the virtue of his name itself, he is the commander in chief of all the natural forces. His invocation at the beginning of any auspicious event provides protection from devils of distraction and destruction.

Worship of Ganesha is practiced all over India. However, a festival is observed that begins by inviting Ganesha into the home. The idol is placed on a pedestal. The place and the surroundings are decorated. Everyday fresh flowers and fine perfume surround. The friends are invited and welcome by offering sweets. Every evening there is singing in the praise of the virtues of Ganesha. This continues at the most for ten days. Finally, the idol is carried to a pond or a river. The immersion and the dissolution of the icon are also celebrated! Last three steps of the meditative process—*Dharana*, *Dhayana* and *Samadhi*—are thus imbibed into the residence for the family.

COMMUNION WITH COSMIC CONSCIOUSNESS: *SAMADHI*

The essence is mentioned with repetition for the sake of emphasis: the glimpse of pristine pure universal Consciousness is obtained by focalizing on a single point with a particular merit. This will gradually eliminate the emanation of ideas from the mental play. Beyond the mental realms, the object that is being meditated upon takes an abstract form. And yet, it is vibrant with a live form. It permeates into each and every cell of the body. Though the processes in the mind are absent there is a dynamic interplay with all the body functions. The molecules of happiness flow in the bloodstream. They rejuvenate and regenerate the body. Disease and illness vanish. This is how the sustained holding of a symbolic form provides sustenance to all the vital planes.

Further flow into a perennial union with cosmic consciousness is a privilege of very few. However, daily practice will provide junction to the unification with cosmic intelligence that ordains all the forces and creates the entire universe. Such a happening is a divine blessing. Here, the observer and the observed have merged. The individual consciousness has discovered its source and the fragment has become the whole. The Nature works with highly specified, well-defined principles. There are no aberrations to the natural laws having had even a glimpse of a union with the fundamental cosmic intelligence, a meditator comes back to perform his functions in daily life in concordance with Nature. There can be a divergence here. A very few may decide to live a life of a recluse. However, they are the ones who are the guiding angels; torch bearers, or a lighthouse. They are in constant communion with cosmic consciousness. Sri Aurobindo called it the descent of super mind. The field of their consciousness, it may be proved with further advancement in quantum physics, may be vast and immense to influence a large mass of humanity.

This is abiding by the Truth that is changeless, eminent and all pervading.

Chapter 9

Epilogue

Yoga and meditation have been utilized as heuristic model to understand the symptom genesis in Ayurveda; it was classically said by Charak as ***Pragnyaparatha jayate sarva rogan that translate as; all diseases arise from faulty functioning of intellect.*** Understanding *Yoga* and meditation and its application in life is of great significance, since life style diseases—perhaps the uniquely human disorders—have been linked with the evolution of the complex faculties for psychodynamics of human brain.

The neuroscientific approaches have to be complemented with concurrent analyses of genome and its recently established correlation with personality types described in Ayurveda. The translational research on the psychoneurobiology of brain and mind following meditative practice are explained. Neurobiological basis of guided meditation that leads to attainment of specific goals is explored. This is correlated with exposure to modern hypnosis and hypnotherapy. The scientific basis of meditation is explained from the use of radio imaging techniques such as functional Magnetic Resonance Imaging (fMRI) and other advance techniques. The empirical evidence for generation of "happy molecules" following meditation is provided. The scientific evidence about selective up regulation and down regulation in meditators of genes is reviewed. This is integrated with the transformation of personality profiles to spiritual aspects as enunciated in Patanjali's *Yoga Sutra*. Further insights in this area would help formulating effective meditative strategies to facilitate happy and healthy mind. It will provide novel intervention strategies to deal with widely prevalent life style diseases.

Exposure is provided to various meditative practices such as Mindfulness Meditation, *Vipassana*, Transcendental Meditation and other practices derived from Kashmir. The practice of Yoga Nidra is taught.

It establishes that meditation is the mother ground of creativity, happiness, health and freedom from disorders. This concise and precise text is meant to inspire the young generation. It will generate new insights for those who have treaded on the path. Regardless of scientific understanding, Nature manifests itself. Science is only 300 years old. Yet, 20th century provided us with intricate interconnection between mind and molecules. Hans Selye and Candace Pert deciphered the molecules of stress and happiness. With bioinformatics, the research is bound to catapult to a state where eliciting a particular thought process may release a cascade of happy molecules. The frontiers for the science of consciousness are still hazy. It will probably need a few more Einsteins and Neil Bohrs to discover the unified theory of four fundamental forces in Nature and, how consciousness can influence and affect matter at a distance.

Bibliography

The Dalai Lama (1999), *Ancient Wisdom, Modern World*, Ethics for a New Millennium, London.

The Dalai Lama (2000), *Transforming the Mind*, Harper Collins Publishers, London.

Doidge, Norman, (2007), *The Brain that Changes Itself*, Penguin Group, USA.

Kaul, Jankinath (1996), 1st edition *Pancastavi*, Leo Printers, New Delhi,

Leadbeater, C.W. & Annie Besant (1905), *Occult Chemistry*, Theosophical Publishing House, Chennai.

Mehta, Rohit (2015), *Yoga The Art of Integration*, Theosophical Publishing House, Chennai.

Phillips, Stephen M. (2006), *ESP of Quarks and Superstrings*, New Age International Ltd., New Delhi.

Rao, K. Ram Krishna, Anand C. Paranjpe, Ajit K. Dala (ed.) (2008), *Handbook of Indian Psychology*, Cambridge University Press India Pvt. Ltd., New Delhi.

Rossi, E.D. Kathryn, Ernest Lawrence Rossi (2012), *Creating Conscicusness*, Milton Erickson Foundation, Paulo Alto, 2012.

Selye, Hans (1956), *Stress of Life*, Bantam Books, New York.

Singh, Jaydev (1978), *Siva Sutra*, Motilal Banarasidass, Varanasi.

Singh, Jaydev (1984), *Vignyan Bhairav*, Motilal Banarasidass, Varanasi.

Sri Aurbindo (2010), reprint *The Integral Yoga*, SABDA Publications, Pondicherry.

Sri Aurbindo (reprint 2004) *Life Divine*, Volume 1 & 2, SABDA Publications, Pondicherry.

Taimini, I.K. (1968), *The Science of Yoga: The Yoga Sutras of Patanjali*, Theosophical Publishing House, Chennai.

Vyas, Bhaskar & D.V. Nene (1994), *Changing Course of Brahmaputra*, Bharatiya Vidhya Bhavan, Mumbai.

Vyas, Bhaskar & Rajni Vyas (2014), *Experiments with Truth & Non-violence: China Challenge*, 2nd Edition, Concept Publishing Company (P) Ltd., New Delhi.

Vyas, Bhaskar & Rajni Vyas, (2017), *Space–Time & Consciousness: The Rationale of Paranormal*, 2nd edition, Concept Publishing Company (P) Ltd., New Delhi.

Vyas, Bhaskar & Rajni Vyas, (2015), (4th Edition) *Indian Handbook of Hypnotherapy*, Concept Publishing Company (P) Ltd., New Delhi.

Index